T0319138

Cambridge Elements ☰

Elements in Digital Literary Studies
edited by
Katherine Bode
Australian National University
Adam Hammond
University of Toronto
Gabriel Hankins
Clemson University

CAN WE BE WRONG? THE PROBLEM OF TEXTUAL EVIDENCE IN A TIME OF DATA

Andrew Piper
McGill University

CAMBRIDGE
UNIVERSITY PRESS

CAMBRIDGE
UNIVERSITY PRESS

University Printing House, Cambridge CB2 8BS, United Kingdom

One Liberty Plaza, 20th Floor, New York, NY 10006, USA

477 Williamstown Road, Port Melbourne, VIC 3207, Australia

314–321, 3rd Floor, Plot 3, Splendor Forum, Jasola District Centre, New Delhi – 110025, India

79 Anson Road, #06–04/06, Singapore 079906

Cambridge University Press is part of the University of Cambridge.

It furthers the University's mission by disseminating knowledge in the pursuit of education, learning, and research at the highest international levels of excellence.

www.cambridge.org
Information on this title: www.cambridge.org/9781108926201
DOI: 10.1017/9781108922036

First published 2020

A catalogue record for this publication is available from the British Library.

ISBN 978-1-108-92620-1 Paperback
ISSN 2633-4399 (online)
ISSN 2633-4380 (print)

Can We Be Wrong? The Problem of Textual Evidence in a Time of Data

Elements in Digital Literary Studies

DOI: 10.1017/9781108922036
First published online: September 2020

Andrew Piper
McGill University
Author for correspondence: andrew.piper@mcgill.ca

Abstract: This Element tackles the problem of generalization with respect to text-based evidence in the field of literary studies. When working with texts, how can we move, reliably and credibly, from individual observations to more general beliefs about the world? The onset of computational methods has highlighted major shortcomings of traditional approaches to texts when it comes to working with small samples of evidence. This Element combines a machine-learning-based approach to detect the prevalence and nature of generalization across tens of thousands of sentences from different disciplines alongside a robust discussion of potential solutions to the problem of the generalizability of textual evidence. It exemplifies the way mixed methods can be used in complementary fashion to develop nuanced, evidence-based arguments about complex disciplinary issues in a data-driven research environment.

Keywords: digital humanities, humanities, machine learning, literary studies, natural language processing

ISBNs: 9781108926201 (PB), 9781108922036 (OC)
ISSNs: 2633-4399 (online), 2633-4380 (print)

Contents

Introduction, or What's Wrong with Literary Studies?

"All of it! – All! – Wilhelm!"
– *The Sorrows of Young Werther*

Over the past few decades, humanists have insisted that it is important to resist generalizations.

The process of secularization associated with modernity has not spread as widely nor penetrated as deeply as Western humanists have tended to assume, not even in the academy.

Without its world, the human is merely another species on earth, testing itself against threats of its own creation and in the process becoming a force like nature (capable only of overt behavior) that jeopardizes its own existence.

Western European philology developed in the eighteenth century at much the same time that the notion of literature did.

The funny thing that happened to charm on its way to modernity was the disenchantment of the West.

Today, anything, it would seem, can be art.

These statements, all drawn from recent academic research in literary studies, represent the tip of a giant methodological iceberg. They signal a much larger and much less well-known problem of what I will be calling the practice of generalization. "Generalization" is the rhetorical strategy whereby we move from partial evidence to knowledge claims about some larger group or category. Whether authors are describing "humanists," "the human," "Western philology," "literature," or simply "art," what these statements all have in common is that they exceed, drastically and exorbitantly, the foundations of what has been observed to make claims about what is.

This Element is about wrestling with this problem, with the gap between what is observed and what is known or, better, believed to be known. While this is a problem for all fields of knowledge, not to mention everyday life, one of the beliefs that I want to explore in this Element is that textual evidence poses distinct challenges for the practice of generalization, of how we move from examples to knowledge. What difference does the weave of written language make when it comes to thinking about the relationship of parts to whole?

The problem of the reliability of textual evidence has emerged with particular urgency today. In what has come to be known as the "reproducibility crisis," we are witnessing a major reassessment of truth claims being made across a number of scientific disciplines (Earp & Trafimow 2015; Spellman 2015). A preponderance of false positives is circulating within scholarly publications – things that are believed to be true but that are not reproducible over time. The increasing failure to reproduce is a sign that the process of generalization, the validity of a belief based on some, but not all, of the evidence has not endured.

At the same time, we are also seeing a widespread concern with the veracity of popular information, which now goes by the colloquial name "fake news." The increasing volume of written communication and the growing speed of circulation through social media have brought with them a similar crisis of verification. Whether in the domain of science or the news, the changing scale of information has foregrounded a basic and recurring problem surrounding the credibility of textual evidence. How can we believe what we read?

The growth of uncertainty surrounding textual evidence is emerging (probably not incidentally) at precisely the same moment as a vast array of new methods and technologies are appearing that claim privileged access to knowledge about texts. Whether under the heading of natural language processing, machine learning, artificial intelligence, or text and data mining, a variety of new techniques have developed over the course of the past decade that aim toward the empirical and quantitative understanding of texts. Scale and measurement are being proposed as an antidote: not simply to the problem of the new (and old) scale of texts but also as a means of repairing the evidentiary deficiencies surrounding the study of texts more generally. But are they the answer we have been looking for?

In plain terms, generalization involves the act of moving from tokens (instances of things) to types (a single representation of a more general category). For example, as a child I saw many trees around me. At a certain point, I developed from these instances the idea of a "tree." As cognitive scientists have shown, generalization is crucial to any learning process (e.g., Erickson & Thiessen 2015; Thiessen 2017). It allows us to dispense with holding many individual representations in our mind in favor of a single, higher-order (more abstract) representation. Instead of maintaining all novels I have read in memory, I create a more general representation of what a novel is in my mind. There is a fundamental utility to generalization. It makes life easier to navigate. Generalizations are also cognitively enabling. They allow us to account for more of our experience with fewer rules.

But generalizations can also be dangerous. It should not be hard for readers to conjure up examples in their minds of disputes they have had with a friend, partner, or child that turned on the issue of an unfair generalization ("that is a total generalization!"). Similarly, one can imagine examples where the persistence of a belief about a particular group (in terms of racial, ethnic, or gender stereotypes, for example) can drive negative behavior toward that group. This is what researchers are concerned about in the case of false positives (i.e., unwarranted generalizations) that can lead to poor social policies (such as unnecessary medical tests) or poor judgments by individuals (such as whether to hire a person or even engage in violence against others). Poor generalizations can make life harder, and potentially more precarious, either for ourselves or for those around us.

The practice of generalization is thus an essential aspect of both social life and knowledge production. How we move from particular observations to more general statements about the world – and the discrepancy between parts and wholes in this process – has an essential bearing on our understanding, our beliefs, and the actions and policies that reflect those beliefs.

This Element sets out to better understand the process of generalization as it pertains to the study of texts. First, what does it mean to generalize about texts and literary texts in particular? What do generalizations look like in literary scholarship? Second, to what extent is this practice happening in our field? How prevalent are the generalizing claims like the ones I cited earlier? Are there particular types of people, journals, or fields where it is happening more (or less) often? And when it is happening, what is the nature and scale of generalization? How can we better understand its scope and qualities? Finally, what, if anything, should we do about it?

My own awareness of the problem of generalization emerged along with the reproducibility crisis in the sciences that began almost a decade ago. Despite a long-term investment in quantitative methods, serious issues were surrounding the credibility of claims being made across a number of different fields. The antidote to the fallibility of generalization had produced its own new set of problems. Numerous reforms were proposed to make scholarship more sound, and yet those calls were not part of the conversation in the humanities. There was a sense of immunity in our field from the evidentiary and methodological problems that surrounded the reproducibility crisis.

Scholars have identified a number of potential causes surrounding the crisis of reproducibility, from small sample sizes, to excessive researcher degrees of freedom, to an absence of transparency with respect to the research process. The more I read around in literary scholarship, including my own past work, the more I began to see how the very problems that were undermining the credibility of claims in the sciences were endemic to literary studies as well. I began to marvel at the discrepancies between researchers' claims, the amount of observations used to make those claims, and the opacity of the methods used to arrive at critical judgments. I will never forget the day I came across this passage by Fredric Jameson:

> Having made these initial distinctions, let me now, by way of a sweeping
> hypothesis, try to say what all third-world cultural productions seem to have
> in common and what distinguishes them radically from analogous cultural
> forms in the first world. All third-world texts are necessarily, I want to argue,
> allegorical, and in a very specific way: they are to be read as what I will call

national allegories, even when, or perhaps I should say, particularly when their forms develop out of predominantly western machineries of representation, such as the novel. (1986, p. 69)

Here Jameson was speaking for *every single* creative work ever produced outside of NATO countries and assigning to them a single distinguishing feature. How could this possibly be true? And how did Jameson think his methods of reading a few books endowed him with the authority to make such sweeping, unverifiable claims? The more I read, the more I saw how pervasive statements like Jameson's were. And in a perverse kind of logic, it was as though the more sweeping and less well justified the claim, the more prestige one could accrue. Did people know what they were doing? And if so, why weren't they concerned?

This Element argues that we should be concerned. By "we" I mean literary scholars across different national literatures, as well as scholars across the humanities for whom methods of case-based research remain their field's primary research method. Generalization is not some esoteric practice that we need not worry about. On the contrary, it is an essential, one might even say existential, scholarly practice that until now has remained all but invisible in critical debates in the humanities. The failure to generalize *well* puts at risk nothing less than our credibility as scholars and cultural commentators.

When it comes to textual evidence, generalization is a problem that can cut two ways. On the one hand, the gap between what has been observed (the examples) and the claims being made (the generalizations) can be so large as to defy belief – as when Jameson speaks for all third-world cultural production or researchers make claims about "the West" or "art" or "the human" and use just a handful of examples to justify their claims. On the other hand, if we take claims to particularity seriously – that we ought to traffic in knowledge of particulars, not generalized beliefs – our knowledge runs the risk of becoming so specific as to be socially meaningless. When we write a whole book or even a single chapter about a single novel, whom or what is this for? What is the social value of knowledge of a single thing?

To better understand the prevalence and nature of generalization within literary studies, this Element applies new techniques of machine learning and natural language processing to study a sample of more than 16,000 statements drawn from recent scholarship in three fields of study (history, sociology, and literary studies).[1] It tries to offer readers one way of structuring an algorithmically informed investigation of texts, in particular as a team-based, interdisciplinary, and even intergenerational undertaking. How can we use machine

---

[1] All data and code can be found at the following repository: https://doi.org/10.6084/m9.fig share.12669329.v1

learning to study complex linguistic phenomena such as generalization? This Element provides a workflow for how to do so, focusing on issues of data collection, conceptual definition, data annotation, and model validation as core aspects of computationally informed textual study.

Based on these methods, the Element's empirical section (Part II) provides evidence for both the consistency and prevalence of generalizing statements within literary studies. Despite calls to the value of particularity that one may hear in the humanities, according to the evidence provided here, scholars in literary studies continue to make generalizing statements with surprising regularity. According to the data presented here, *an estimated one out of every two or three sentences* in the framing of research articles is predicted to be a generalization, on par with a far more quantitative field like sociology. Delving more deeply into the data, we can also see how the conceptual scales at which researchers are working are both vast and apparently growing.

The findings uncovered here raise a host of challenging questions, not just for literary studies but also for the humanities more generally. Given the glaring discrepancies between the scale of claims being made and the amount of evidence being used to support these claims, what should we do about it?

This is obviously a challenging question to answer, and I can only begin to sketch some possible ways forward here. In the discussion section (Part III), I entertain but ultimately eschew two simpler and more straightforward arguments: (1) we should either *not* be generalizing at all because this is not what literary scholarship does or (2) we should *only* be generalizing because this is the very definition of scholarship (in the German sense of *Wissenschaft*, a body of knowledge) and therefore we require a massive overhaul of our methods to move largely away from case-based research. As I will discuss at greater length, the latter is an idealization that overlooks the irreducibility of textual meaning, that there can be no final validity of what a text or group of texts *means*. There are basic and fundamental limits to the universality of truth claims that can be made when it comes to questions of textual meaning and our ability to model and measure them. This is the first "problem of textual evidence" that I invoke in my title.

At the same time, the former position (that we should not be generalizing at all) is an idealization that overlooks our own behavior. As this Element will demonstrate, the practice of generalization is widespread in the scholarly literature. The generalization that we do not generalize is, according to the data presented here, a very poor generalization. But the resistance to the value of generalization itself also overlooks a vibrant tradition of scholarship within the field's history where the arrival at generalizable knowledge about texts is an essential aspect of the project of textual understanding. From Lorenzo Valla and early humanists to the nineteenth-century rise of hermeneutics to today's textual forensics (Iqbal et al. 2013), avoiding misinterpretation has been a central value of the field of textual study for centuries. At a time when misinformation has become a primary social ill, developing methods that generate confidence in textual meaning is arguably more important than ever. This is the second sense by which I mean the "problem of textual evidence." How can we develop methods that move beyond the often incredible gaps between observation and interpretation that are operative in the field today?

In place of these two more extreme positions, I argue instead for two more moderate ways forward, each of which is premised on differing notions of "openness." The first asks us to move from questions of evidentiary sufficiency – when is some evidence *enough* – to questions of evidentiary transparency – how much of the research process has been explicated? Given that we can never have all of the evidence before us, in either qualitative *or* quantitative scholarship, how can we make more explicit all of the tools, techniques, and procedures that were undertaken to arrive at our general statements about the world? My aim here is to move past a two-cultures approach to evidence, where quantitative and qualitative methods operate and are valued according to different evidentiary criteria. Drawing on recent work that has emphasized principles of transparency surrounding scholarship in the name of "open science" (Willinsky 2006; Stodden, Guo, & Ma 2013; Foster & Deardorff 2017; Vincente-Saez & Martinez-Fuentes 2018), I argue that these principles need to be embodied more fully within humanistic disciplines like literary studies. While we have made (some) strides in the area of open access with respect to publishing, we have not addressed the accessibility and openness of our methods, evidence, and modes of judgment in equal measure. Using this Element's approach as a model, I provide suggestions for ways that *all* scholarship in literary studies can implement more open evidentiary procedures. If we are going to continue to make generalizations about how documents in the world work at the rate at which we are currently making them, we need to address the evidentiary and methodological elisions of our methods. The result will ideally be a good deal more moderation with respect to the claims being made in case-based research, what we might call a new culture of limitation.

The second moderate pathway argues that instead of seeing all literary scholarship as invested only and ever in making generalized claims about how texts work, that we take seriously the idea of the contingency of textual interpretation whose roots go back at least as far as Immanuel Kant. No amount of sampling or predictive modeling will ever fully explicate once and for all the question of textual meaning. While the problem of the irreducibility of truth claims is endemic to all fields of knowledge (Reichenbach 1930; Popper 1935), a long tradition of research in literary studies has drawn attention to the way the solicitation of multiple and subjective responses to texts is not a problem to be minimized but the fundamental purpose of the discipline. As I will show in this section, in addition to the prevalence of generalization within the field, we can also find evidence for the ways in which scholarship in literary studies is indeed more conceptually and rhetorically open than work in the sciences. This is the second notion of openness that I want to emphasize here, not in the sense of transparency and visibility, but as a form of novelty and unknownness. To return to my earlier question, what is the value of engaging deeply with single things, this section argues that it can serve as a mechanism for producing a more interrogative and expansive mind-set.

Rather than seeing this practice as the *only* value of textual study however – as oppositional to the project of generalization and knowledge production – my argument is that we would benefit by envisioning these two strains of research in more complementary ways. Seeing and celebrating the critical project of particularism as something partial rather than universal will not only help us better account for what we are actually doing in our scholarship. It will also help us see the relational value between these two methodological modes. The conceptual openness of literary scholarship – its exploration of the hypothetical, from possible worlds to potential ideas – can be an ideal companion to inform more nuanced, creative, and flexible generalizations about the textual worlds that we study. I want us to see the value of *mutuality* between the conceptual openness of literary scholarship and the methodological openness of generalizing about how the world works.

To be clear, my goal in writing this Element is not to put forward a normative account of the discipline of literary studies, a single vision of what literary studies is and does. It is too diverse a thing for a single account. Rather, my aim is to better understand the alignment (or in this case misalignment) between our discursive practices and epistemic ideals, what we say in our work and what we hope to know through it. In this, I see it as part of a long tradition of work in disciplinary self-assessment, what James Evans and Jacob Foster (2011) have called a form of "metaknowledge." Work by John Guillory (1993), Gauri Viswanathan (1989), Rachel Buurma and Laura Heffernan (2012), Merve Emre (2018), and Chad Wellmon and Paul Reitter (forthcoming, 2021) are just a few of the many valuable works that have used extensive archival research to highlight the ways in which institutional and political contexts shape disciplinary behavior. In using a computational approach, my hope is that this Element can serve as a model for future large-scale studies of disciplinary behavior, following in the footsteps of important precedents (Goldstone & Underwood

2014; Wellmon & Piper 2017; Degaetano-Ortlieb & Piper 2019; Bourrier & Thelwall 2020).

Many of the recent debates surrounding the future of literary studies have often been technologically inflected – whether one can or cannot arrive at insights about literature using one kind of technology (computation) or another (bibliographic). Or they have been invested in trying to define the particular nature of knowledge unique to literary studies as distinct (or not) from other disciplines. My goal here is to move us away from discussions about the kind of knowledge we produce to a study of the *relationships* between the kinds of evidence we use and the discursive procedures that make that evidence visible to others.

After several years of thinking about this problem and discussing it with others, I have also become aware just how complicated and nuanced the problem is. The practice of generalization is not something that can be solved within a single book or from a single point of view. Indeed, it cannot be "solved" in any strict sense. It represents an ongoing state that requires regular and collective action, from the changing habits of individual researchers to the policies of editors and editorial boards with respect to peer review. The work of generalization is by definition never finished. My hope with this Element is to start an important conversation.

I Theory

1 Generally Speaking

From Exemplarity to Estimation

In the paper that would ultimately gain him admission to the French Academy of Sciences, "Mémoire sur la probabilité des causes par les évènements" (1774), Pierre Simon Laplace asked whether given a large number of astronomical observations that all differed from one another, there was a way to derive the true, or at least most confident, location of a planet traversing the heavens. Laplace's aim was to develop a mathematical model to understand the relationship of observation to error, that is, to think probabilistically about the nature of events in the world.

Laplace's work represented a watershed moment in the history of ideas. It attempted for the first time to formalize an understanding of the distribution of observations as a means of thinking about accuracy and truth. Rather than rely on a single best example, Laplace's method attempted to consider a *set* (or in modern-day parlance a *sample*) of observations and produce a single best estimate. While all observations were not imagined to be equally valid (the further away they were from some imagined midpoint, the more likely they were to be erroneous, or so Laplace theorized), neither was any one of them categorically assumed to be "the best." It marked an important beginning in the process of formalizing uncertainty and error as *part* of knowledge and truth rather than as enemies of it. Instead of emphasizing a single observation, Laplace's model provided a method to understand the relationship of observations to each other. It replaced exemplarity with estimation.

Laplace's initial mathematical solution to estimating the distribution of error was, it turned out, in error (Stigler 1986). Understanding effective ways to model the distribution and potential error of observations was a complex mathematical problem that would gradually evolve over a number of years. Like all scholarly debates, it entailed an active social process of argument and publication. Laplace's own work built on earlier investigations by Johann Lambert, Joseph Lagrange, and Thomas Bayes. The German mathematician Carl Friedrich Gauss would eventually provide the solution to what came to be known as the "normal" distribution in 1809.

Over the course of four decades, then, roughly equivalent to one academic career, a profoundly new way of understanding nature had emerged. Instead of relying on a single "best" observation – a model based on an authoritative observer – scholars were putting into place a new model that took into account numerous observations to infer an "ideal" observation. In one sense, both practices involved forms of idealization. The exemplary example was an ideal version of its kind, just as the inferred estimate based on a sample of observations was. But according to the latter model, the accuracy of one's insight depended on an understanding of the *relationship* of observations to each other rather than on a single, arbitrarily representative body.

The story of how such probabilistic thinking would gradually penetrate numerous fields of knowledge over the course of the nineteenth century is by now well known (Porter 1986), though much of its twentieth- and twenty-first-century continuation still remains to be written. Also well known is the extent to which scholars in the humanities have largely, though not exclusively, resisted this transition.[2] Literary scholars have continued to overwhelmingly rely on methods that depend on an authoritative observer choosing the "best" observation(s) to prove some larger point.

---

[2] In a sample of the first 100 articles listed in the Modern Language Association database from different journals filtered according to the subject heading "English literature" on April 28, 2020, only 1 article used quantitative methods. In the journal *American Sociological Review* for 2016 drawn from this Element's sample, by contrast, 43 of 47 articles were quantitative in nature. Our working understanding of the prevalence of quantitative and computational work in the field of literary studies is thus ~ 1 percent of research outputs. Future work can provide more accurate estimates.

The new availability of increasing amounts of textual data along with a variety of computational methods to analyze that data has allowed literary scholars to begin to follow in the footsteps of Laplace and utilize the same practices of generalizability as other disciplines. So why haven't we embraced these methods more broadly? And should we be doing so?

The Curse of Lorenzo Valla

In 1440, Lorenzo Valla completed his *Oration on the Falsely-Believed and Forged Donation of Constantine*. As the title of his self-described *opusculum* or "little work" announced, Valla claimed to have proven that the decree composed by the Emperor Constantine in the fourth century that transferred authority over the Roman Empire to the pope was false. As Valla wrote to one of his interlocutors, "Why did I write about the Donation of Constantine? . . . For the sake of truth" (cited in Camporeale 1996, p. 9.).

Valla's oration is consistently held up as one of the primary examples of the intellectual contributions of Renaissance humanism, what Donald Kelley later called "the historical revolution" in textual criticism (1970). As scholars have long pointed out, doubt about the Donation was hardly new (Bowersock 2008). What was new was the historical method that Valla applied to disprove the document's authenticity. Valla took aim at the language and logic of the decree by showing how incongruous it was with the surrounding documents of its age. "You say that within the first few days the Senate, the nobles, and the satraps [i.e. provincial governors], as though already Christians, passed decrees with the Caesar for honoring the Roman church! What! . . . Whoever heard of satraps being mentioned in the councils of Romans?" (Valla 2008, p. 85). Valla's extensive knowledge of ancient documents allowed him to identify these linguistic anachronisms, just as his sensitivity to language allowed him to ascertain when words belonged to a source that could not have been known by Constantine: "Constantine is made to arrogate himself the titles of God, and to try to imitate the language of the sacred scriptures, which he had never read" (Valla 2008, pp. 91–93). For Valla, detailed attention to the style and vocabulary of documents, what we would now call techniques of "close reading," allowed him to, if not prove the actual date of composition, then at least falsify claims surrounding the document's date of composition and thus its institutional validity.

Valla's case has become celebrated as a heroic instance of when close reading was successfully used to challenge the claims of power. For Valla's disciples, his methods would become a foundation of humanist scholarship (Nauta 2009). From the subsequent editorial work of Erasmus, who sought to produce reliable print editions of Greek and Latin classics, through nineteenth-century figures like Karl Lachmann, who aimed to produce "critical" editions of early German texts, to twentieth-century figures like Fredson Bowers and his theory of the "copy-text," a tradition of literary scholarship has for more than five centuries focused on establishing the veracity of texts and the reliability of the textual record (Reynolds & Wilson 1991; Grafton 1994; Lerer 2002). And scholars have done so using methods pioneered by Lorenzo Valla.

Valla's methods have been central not only to the work of bibliography and textual criticism, however. As scholars have pointed out, they were also central to the tradition of hermeneutics and the project of textual understanding that emerged toward the beginning of the nineteenth century (Fohrmann & Voßkamp 1994). For Friedrich Schleiermacher, considered to be one of the founders of the modern tradition of textual interpretation, understanding something *correctly*, what Schleiermacher called "the art of understanding the speech of another correctly [*die Kunst, die Rede eines andern richtig zu verstehen*]," presupposed that you could also *misunderstand* a person's speech (1977, p. 75). My statements about another person's statements could be wrong. And according to Schleiermacher, such correct understanding depended upon knowledge of the contextual whole to which any individual text belonged. As Schleiermacher would write in words that were deeply informed by the methods and assumptions of Lorenzo Valla, "Every act of speech can thus only be understood through knowledge of the historical life-totality to which it belongs [*Jede Rede kann ferner nur verstanden werden durch die Kenntnis des geschichtlichen Gesamtlebens, wozu sie gehört*]" (1977, p. 77). Being right about a text's meaning was conditional upon some generalized knowledge of the whole.

Valla's contemporaries did not universally accept his emphasis on historical method (Grafton & Jardine 1986; Nauta 2009; Wellmon & Reitter forthcoming 2021). This should come as no surprise. New methods never are. But the idea that a technical method focused on historical truth could replace a notion of timeless truth grounded in the moral exemplarity of one's source (and by extension its interpreter) was seen as fundamentally misguided. Valla's exclusive focus on empirical rather than moral truth – his tenacious emphasis on *proof* itself – was, then as now, a contested position.

And yet proof about the veracity of his source text was not Valla's only concern, neither was the philological analysis of language his only method (Camporeale 1996). Not only did Valla argue by way of omission – surely, he suggested, there should be some other recording of this monumental historical event than a single piece of parchment ("What an infinite number of coins of the supreme pontiffs would be found if you ever had ruled Rome!"). He also argued by way of imagination. The opening third of the document was framed not as an extended exhibit of close reading but the emulation of what historical actors would *likely* have said under the circumstances: "Who would not acknowledge himself moved by the speech of Sylvester, that is, if the event had ever actually occurred. It would doubtless have been something like this." The force of Valla's argument in this case was framed not by the contradictory evidence of the text and its context but by the imitation of laudable Roman discourse. In other words, to disprove a bad forgery, a good forgery was the best kind of evidence! Because one could never know *for certain* that the document was fake, Valla turned to, indeed opened with, another kind of evidence: persuasion and the creative power of language.

Valla is a useful example for my purposes here because of the way his work highlights competing evidentiary tensions that surrounded the study of texts during one of the field's key founding moments, tensions that are, as I will endeavor to show, still very much with us. On the one hand, we can identify unambiguous claims to truth and falsehood being made in Valla's treatise with respect to the meaning of texts. Valla and his opponents can be wrong. And yet we also have an unambiguous emphasis on the rhetorical primacy of evidence – that the goal is not simply to prove, but to *persuade*. Imagination emerges not just as one more value of the treatise's methods, but the primary value. No matter how detailed Valla's philological methods, there would always be an element of unverifiability to the textual truth he was after. Fully aware that he would never be able to entirely validate his claims, Valla turned first and foremost to the power of persuasion, to the power of *belles-lettres*. And yet despite or perhaps precisely because of these contradictions, there emerged both short- and long-term consensus that Valla was right (and not wrong). We continue to believe to this day that the decree was a forgery.

What I am calling the "curse" of Lorenzo Valla, then, is the way these two opposing methodological aspects that coexist in Valla's work do so in an undifferentiated way. According to Valla's model, belief in the truth of something is a function of two very different kinds of evidence: empirical observations on the one hand and the power of exemplary words on the other. And yet these two very different modes of evidence are presented not in a complementary way, where one informs the other, but as *interchangeable*. Where one falls short, the other is brought to bear. Valla silently moves from one mode to the other, with no indication of the vastly different principles underlying each. Rhetoric is all-too-conveniently swapped in for evidence.

If we want to understand why literary scholars (and humanists more generally) have been slow to embrace Laplace's paradigm, I would suggest it is because there has existed, for well over five centuries, a competing set of values associated not with proof and generalization, but with the importance of rhetoric and creativity. But rather than represent an exclusive and distinct paradigm of knowledge, these values have, as in Valla's work and as I will show in Part II, comingled with the values of empirical, evidence-based generalizations about the world. Moral exemplarity – the value(s) of the speaker – has served as the ultimate backstop for evidentiary sufficiency – the value of generalization(s). Escaping the curse of Lorenzo Valla means more clearly recognizing these different dimensions of literary scholarship and imagining ways they can more productively inform one another.

The Reproducibility Crisis and the Future of Literary Scholarship

In November 2012, the newly created Open Science Collaboration (OSC) published a brief article announcing a multiyear effort to "estimate the reproducibility of psychological science" (Open Science Collaboration 2012). Brian Nosek of the University of Virginia directed the collaboration, which would eventually involve more than 250 coauthors. According to the collaboration, reproducibility was one of, if not the single most defining feature of, the social endeavor known as "science." "Other types of belief," the authors write, "depend on the authority and motivations of the source; beliefs in science do not" (Open Science Collaboration 2012, p. 657). The ability to reproduce scientific results across time and space – the ability to have results be *independent* of the individuals involved – is what made science scientific according to the OSC. And yet, the findings of the reproducibility project, which were published two and half years later in 2015, showed a remarkable reproductive failure.[3] The very value upon which science was supposed to be founded appeared to be an exception rather than a norm.

The OSC's article would become one of the foundational documents in what has colloquially come to be known as the "reproducibility crisis" in science (Earp & Trafimow 2015; Spellman 2015). Numerous high-profile cases from biomedicine to economics to social psychology have emerged over the past decade where important findings have subsequently been unable to be reproduced (Baggerly & Combes 2009; Ash, Herndon, & Pollin 2013). Despite these fields' investment in Laplace's vaunted probabilistic framework, it turned out that the reliability of their insights was called deeply into question. Quantification had not *by itself* insulated these fields from misbelief.

---

[3] According to the authors of the report, "Ninety-seven percent of original studies had significant results (p < 0.05). Thirty-six percent of replications had significant results; 47% of original effect sizes were in the 95% confidence interval of the replication effect size" (Open Science Collaboration 2015).

In undertaking their project, however, the aim of the OSC was not to invalidate the quantitative methods underlying their field's work, to put an end, once and for all, to Laplace's folly. Rather, their aim was to draw attention to the value of reproducibility and associated concepts like "transparency" and "openness" as core frameworks for doing research. As the authors write:

> After this intensive effort to reproduce a sample of published psychological findings, how many of the effects have we established are true? Zero. And how many of the effects have we established are false? Zero. Is this a limitation of the project design? No. It is the reality of doing science. (2015, p. 7)

According to the OSC, there was no way to fully validate *or* falsify, once and for all, a theoretical claim. What mattered instead, coming all the way back to Laplace, was the idea of *confidence*. In words that echoed influential positions in the philosophy of science that would emerge in response to the "crisis of relativity" initiated by Albert Einstein in the early twentieth century (Reichenbach 1930; Popper 1935), the OSC authors write, "Scientific progress is a cumulative process of uncertainty reduction that can only succeed if science itself remains the greatest skeptic of its explanatory claims" (Open Science Collaboration 2015, p. 7). As the physicist and philosopher Hans Reichenbach posited almost a century earlier:

> We have called the principle of induction the vehicle for the condition of truth [*Wahrheitsentscheid*] within science. To be more precise we ought to say that it serves the condition of probability [*Wahrscheinlichkeitsentscheid*]. Truth and falsehood are not the opposing alternatives of science; rather, for scientific statements there are only continual degrees of probability, whose unreachable boundaries are truth and falsehood. (1930, p. 186)

When the second OSC paper initially appeared, its value was often framed through the lens of scientific failure. Like Valla several centuries earlier, they successfully debunked the false claims of a privileged elite. And yet the authors were very careful to emphasize that the true value of their undertaking was the undertaking itself, not the validity of their findings or the invalidity of those that they studied. The value of the OSC project was the notion of reproducibility itself and the way it aligned the concept of truth, that is, the ability to make valid general claims about the world, with notions of confidence and social consensus. With their 250 coauthors and a host of reproductive methods, the OSC emphasized the shared nature and temporal communicability of knowledge, the way validity was a function not of individual exemplarity, but of collective practices over time. They manifested, explicitly and forthrightly, that knowledge is a social construction (Shapin 1994; Hacking 1999).

The OSC project represents one of the most important recent interventions in the long history of scientific self-assessment. It has had a profound impact on a variety of disciplines' self-understanding, leading to numerous recommendations for improving the practice of building scholarly consensus about different forms of knowledge. To date, however, its effects have not been felt in the field of literary studies or, indeed, any other humanistic disciplines. And yet the very problems that have been identified as potential sources of the reproducibility crisis are endemic to research in literary studies, too. These include the lack of shared data (such as researcher notes regarding records consulted or unreproducible archives); researcher "degrees of freedom" (Nelson, Simmons, & Simonsohn 2011) to manipulate experimental settings to arrive at the most favorable outcomes (such as the lack of transparency surrounding methodological choices in selecting and interpreting documents); small sample sizes (N=?); and the positivity bias of academic publication (Horbat, Mlinarić, & Smolčić 2017), that is, the way literary scholars never report *not* finding something. All of these practices belong to the trade of literary studies.

The OSC project thus provides a timely opportunity to reconsider a host of evidentiary practices in our field as they relate to the aim of producing generalizable claims about the world. The principles of openness, transparency, and as we will see moderation that inform the idea of open science offer a new kind of foundation from which we can begin to close the credibility gap in our scholarship. As I will outline in the following sections, these ideals offer a blueprint for how to move from a model of exemplary truths – those based on the moral (or intellectual) superiority of the statement's source (this is right because I say so) – to a model of truth as a function of social confidence – this is right because *we* believe it is *likely* the case.

Skeptics might argue that we need not worry about these concerns because we don't or shouldn't generalize. There can be no reproducibility crisis if reproducibility doesn't matter. We don't traffic in general claims about the world and therefore do not require consensus about their validity. As the chair of the International Committee in Humanities Higher Education Group declared, "Particularise ... that is what the humanities do – mount arguments from particulars and highlight and give narratives to the singular" (cited in Levine 2017, p. 633). The problem with this argument is that besides being tantalizingly paradoxical (as one generalizes about the value of particularizing), this belief does not adequately capture actual researcher behavior. As I will show in Part II, researchers appear to generalize with great frequency. While they may mount arguments from particulars, they use those particulars to make remarkably general claims, claims that also appear to have grown considerably in their generality over time. The generalization that humanists particularize is, according to the data presented here, a particularly poor generalization.

Others might argue that generalization is indeed important but that there is nothing wrong with the evidence we are using to do so. If other experts deem our evidence sufficient through the process of peer review, then that should be enough. But as I will try to show in Part II, the scale at which our claims are being made is so large as to defy any sense of credibility. There can be no way that a handful of examples could ever sufficiently account for generalizations about categories as vast as the human, the reader, the Enlightenment, or postwar fiction (to name just a few). Making normative claims about the world only by way of examples is a moral, not knowledge-based enterprise. As I illustrate in Section 3, these evidentiary holes lead to a host of conceptual and rhetorical short circuits that elide the evidentiary shortcomings endemic to our claims. The notion of "open generalization" put forth in Section 4 is thus a way to make these elisions more transparent, whether for qualitative or quantitative work. All research operates according to a fundamental leap between observation and inference. The aim of open generalization is to close the credibility gap surrounding our field's current practices and institute a culture of limitation and moderation as it relates to generalization, especially when it comes to case-based research.

Does that mean we should do away entirely with case-based research? Of course not. Numerous values potentially reside in the close encounter with particular observations. Examples can facilitate understanding or affective attachment, which may lead to behavioral or psychological change (whether for the better is a different matter). In Section 5, I zoom in on one of these particular values. As I try to show, when compared with other fields of knowledge, literary scholarship appears to invest more heavily in rhetorical tactics that harken back to Valla's initial project and its focus on creativity and the imagination. In addition to the frequent use of generalizations, literary studies' detailed engagement with particular examples also produces far more rhetorically and conceptually open language. Placing all of the emphasis on generalization and evidentiary sufficiency misses the other side of Valla's methodological coin.

Instead of seeing these two positions as mutually exclusive, my aim in this Element is to begin to help us see how they can more productively inform each other. The first step in that process is acknowledging their different priorities and aims. Rather than continue to operate according to a substitution model, where rhetoric stands in for evidence, where interestingness becomes true (or the truth is only valued because it is interesting), we need to more clearly signal what our aims are with respect to our evidence. If our aim is to produce generalizable beliefs about the world, then we need better practices with respect to openness, transparency, and moderation as envisioned by the OSC. But if our aim is to engender more creative thinking about the world – to open ourselves up to the unthought and the unseen – we need a way to link this up with the process of generalization without it surreptitiously becoming the subsequent basis of evidentiary claims. Reproducibility is by itself too narrow a concept to capture the ways in which we build confidence about how complex things in the world work. Imagination has a key role to play in the process, too. Work that fosters that imaginative landscape is thus intrinsically valuable to the research process.

In his *Logic of Scientific Discovery*, Karl Popper argued that the goal of science was not "the preservation of untenable systems, but the selection of the most relatively tenable through the strictest possible form of competition" (1935, p.14). I would posit the exact opposite axiom as equally important for literary study, if not all endeavors of knowledge production: not the selection of the most tenable system, but the explicit production of *untenable* systems, the imagination of all possible and impossible worlds. This is another value of openness that our field can contribute to the larger landscape of knowledge creation. How can the untenable and the hypothetical be used to inform our efforts at better understanding the world around us?

II Evidence

2 Modeling and Machine Learning

Building a Team, Building a Model

The fundamental question guiding this Element is to ask how and to what extent scholars in literary studies generalize. Before advocating for different evidentiary practices, we need to first understand the current state of affairs. Do we, in the words of one scholar, "resist generalizations" (Levine 2017, p. 633) ? Is this a fair generalization of the field?

To try to provide an answer to this question, this Element takes advantage of new computational methods in text analysis. While the close engagement with numerous examples will be central to understanding the problem, the power of sample-based methods will be used for the purposes of generalization. To have a general understanding of the practice of generalization, we need some way of estimating its widespread behavior. The aim of this and the following sections is to provide a blueprint for answering such complex conceptual questions with respect to texts using the processes of machine learning and natural language processing.

The first step involves assembling a team of researchers from different disciplines and different academic levels. Doing so allows us to try to transcend individual as well as disciplinary biases and blind spots. If we want to have a generalizable understanding of the practice of generalization, then it follows that more diverse points of view that participate in the modeling process will help make resulting models more generally applicable.

Our team consisted of three faculty members, three undergraduate students, and one graduate student, drawn from the disciplines of literary studies, art history, biomedical ethics, cultural studies, linguistics, history, and computer science. As this list should indicate, it is at once broad and also selective. Having more researchers does not by itself guarantee that one will intrinsically transcend bias anymore than having more data will intrinsically overcome problems of selection bias. At the same time, the breadth of expertise, education, and discipline meant that our discussions were informed by very different experiences and assumptions. While we do not provide records here of our meetings (a potential consideration for future work), based on my own anecdotal experience I can say I was profoundly impacted and impressed by the tumultuous, vibrant, and evolving nature of our discussions. I for one did not end even close to where I started in my thinking about this issue.

To move from the practices of discussion and consensus building to that of analysis, I use the term "modeling" to capture the diverse forms of mediation that connect the conceptual stages of the project with the analytical (Piper 2017). As one of the collaborators on the project had previously written, models are simulations, a combination of technique and technology that aims to represent the world in some way but also reduce its complexity (Hunter 2010). As the famous quip goes, "all models are wrong" (So 2017). The question is not whether a model perfectly represents the world, but as Gabriele Contessa (2007) has argued, the ways in which models facilitate potentially valid inferences about the world: "Faithful epistemic representation is a matter of degree. A vehicle does not need to be a completely faithful representation of its target in order to be an epistemic representation of it" (p. 55).

One of the challenges of machine learning that I will discuss when it comes to modeling and interpretation is the problem of *explication* (Rudin 2019). In machine learning, the model being used to represent some textual phenomenon is not readily reducible to a single equation or measurement. For example, if we wanted to create a model of "vocabulary richness," we could use the formula of type-token ratio, which divides the number of word types by the number of word tokens. We can readily explicate the conditions through which such a model arrives at judgments about texts. Machine learning by contrast is based on learning a complex representation of a phenomenon built upon a collection of examples. What exactly has been learned and what is being conditioned upon in the algorithm's judgments remain more opaque. It is for this reason that we need to undertake both pre- and post-model efforts to explicate and understand our model, that is, to make as transparent as possible the steps that were taken to build it and the qualities that are being inferred based upon it. This is the priority – and irreducibility – of the principle of openness that I talked about in Part I. It is an ideal that can never be fully reached because tacit knowledge will always be built into the model and the "epistemic representation" it produces (Polanyi 2009). The point is to maximize the openness surrounding the inferential process.

To proceed I will be following the following five steps of model building adapted from Piper 2017:

1. Definition. Defining our concept consists of establishing a "shared understanding" of the problem among our team. What do we mean by generalization and why is it important? This process can consist of drawing upon existing theories, engagement with numerous examples, or some combination thereof. In our case, it meant several weeks of reading and discussing primary literature, for example, recent academic articles in the field of literary studies, with an eye to how and when authors made statements that we considered to be "generalizations." Close reading and seminar-like discussions were the primary methods used during this phase. The outcome of this phase was the production of an annotation guide, often referred to as a "codebook," which explicates our definition of the problem using positive and negative examples, which we reproduce in the following section and in the supplementary data. In some sense, one could see this phase as encompassing the whole process of close reading. Reflection is expended on a problem and examples are provided that are meant to illuminate and define that problem. But rather than stop there and start generalizing, computational methods undertake a series of further steps to ensure greater transparency and representativeness when it comes to the conclusions that are drawn from evidence.

2. Selection. The next step is creating a "sample" of evidence drawn from some larger population, in this case articles drawn from the field of literary studies (as well as two other disciplines for comparative purposes). In many cases, generating a truly random sample (i.e., "probability sample") of some population is extremely challenging (Bode 2018, 2020). This is the case when it comes to academic documents. In some cases, a random sample may not be desirable (as when one is interested in studying more prestigious or more circulated material). But in others, it may not be possible, as in the case of unclear boundaries of the population (where does a discipline "end"?). Here we follow the sampling

procedure of the OSC paper (Open Science Collaboration 2015), which conditions on the idea of "leading" journals in the field from a single synchronic slice of time. The important point to keep in mind is that sampling not only allows us to base our estimates off of more and potentially more representative examples than traditional methods. It also makes the process of evidentiary selection more transparent. For sure, hundreds of examples of something are far better than just "a few" if you want to generalize. But there is no guarantee that potential biases are not encoded in the selection of data that may change one's estimation of the problem. The important point is that sampling allows for future work to test the validity of the conclusions drawn by adjusting the sampling (or modeling) procedure. Rather than argue that sample X is biased because it does not include some quality Y and is therefore invalid, we need to be able to demonstrate the effects of biases on our estimates of the problem. As the OSC paper is at pains to argue, we are not definitively proving or disproving something when we sample from some population, but we are gaining confidence about our beliefs in the problem's general validity. In our case, we undertake a series of steps to capture data that is both representative of something (in this case literary studies) and also stratified into different subsets to potentially capture differences of degree, including collecting data from outside the field to provide extra-disciplinary benchmarks.

3. Annotation. Because machine learning learns by examples, referred to as a form of "supervised" learning, we need to institute some procedure for the annotation of both positive and negative examples and a procedure to assess the generality of those annotations. In some cases, such annotations already exist in the world and can be collected (e.g., library classification codes for certain kinds of documents). In others, as in our case, we need to generate these annotations manually. As readers will see, we use a hybrid model that relies on annotations by a single disciplinary expert (me) that are validated against a team of nonexperts. Different annotation processes can be used depending on the research aims of a project, but the key dimension is to assess the generalizability of these annotations. How much would others agree with an annotation and how much ambiguity is there in the process? Again, there are no right answers. The point is to make visible how much uncertainty informs the estimates provided.

4. Implementation. Once we have the definition of our concept, the selection of data to be studied, and the annotation of examples, we can then implement our machine learning model(s). As with every step, this step involves recording as many of the parameters used as possible and showing the relative performance of different model choices. It is important to see what the algorithmic criteria are for the estimates that are ultimately provided. The model first learns a

representation of the textual phenomenon (in this case generalization) based on the annotated data and then predicts whether or not unseen statements belong to this category.

5. Validation. Finally, we arrive at a second and third stage of validation (as we have already validated the reliability of the annotations themselves). The second level of validation involves a straightforward assessment of the model's predictive accuracy. Based on our "true" annotations, how well was the model able to identify whether or not a statement belonged to the category we call "generalization"? Here we use the process of x-fold validation, where multiple rounds of prediction are run on the same training data, which are partitioned into training and test data (called folds). But validation also consists of assessing what the model is predicting when it predicts a particular category. This step involves looking more closely at the nature of statements that have been predicted to be generalizations compared to those that are not. It is in this stage that we use follow-up forms of text and data analysis to generalize about the nature of the generalizations that the machine learning process has learned. It provides insights into the nature of our model and at the same time the nature of the problem *as we have come to understand it.*

For the purposes of transparency, we list each of our roles with respect to the different phases. All members participated in the definition phase. Emma Ebowe, Victoria Svaikovsky, Nicholas King, and Andrew Piper participated in the annotation phase. Eve Kraicer was responsible for the data selection and the preparation of data for the annotation and annotation-validation phases. Sunyam Bagga was responsible for the implementation of the machine learning model and its validation. Andrew Piper was responsible for the final validation phase and the writing of this Element. I am deeply appreciative of all team members for the time they took to contribute to this project.

That's a Generalization!

So what does it mean "to generalize"? According to the OED, *to generalize* means "to convert (an idea, perception, etc.) into a general concept or rule; to broaden the application of." The first known use of the verb "generalize" in this sense was by George Berkeley in his *Treatise Concerning the Principles of Human Knowledge* (1710): "the making use of Words, implies the having of general Ideas. From which it follows, that men who use Language are able to Abstract or Generalize their Ideas." (The first use I could discover was in Daniel Rogers' *Naaman the Syrian, His Disease and Cure* from 1650, where he writes how "our base spirits are content to generalize with God.") Berkeley's treatise was written in response to Locke's *Essay on Human Understanding* (1690), which posed the fundamental question: "Since all things that exist are only Particulars, how come we by general Terms?"

Berkeley was unhappy with Locke's solution that "general and universal belong not to the real existence of things; but are the inventions and creatures of the understanding, made by it for its own use, and concern only signs, whether words or ideas" (1824, B3.C3.P11). For Locke, generalization was simply a matter of denotation: a word signified a general idea or did not depending on how it was used. Berkeley, on the other hand, insisted that such general terms were *fundamentally linked* with particular observations upon which they depended. "I believe," writes Berkeley, "we shall acknowledge, that an Idea, which consider'd in itself is particular, becomes general, by being made to represent or stand for all other particular Ideas of the same sort" (1710, p. 17).

Berkeley's response to Locke is a useful framework for understanding generalization because it establishes two important principles that will be operative in our analysis here. The first is that generalization is a linguistic phenomenon – it is something that is expressed through a *particular* use of language. Generalization belongs to a "sort" or "class" of language and is thus distinguishable from other kinds of language use.

The second important point is that generalization is not only a language game – a choice of how to use words – but one that depends on a *relationship* between a set of words (signifiers) and the real-world objects to which these signifiers refer. Understanding generalization as a practice means understanding both the linguistic cues that underpin it as well as the relations it establishes to the set of particular observations upon which it is based.

In what follows, we focus first on developing a process for identifying the linguistic conditions of generalizing statements within literary critical discourse. Generalizing statements should not be understood as simply one more type of statement that belongs to academic research – that is, as simply interchangeable or complementary to other statements – but instead as hierarchically superior to other kinds of statements. As Karl Popper writes in *The Logic of Scientific Discovery*, "The activity of the scientific researcher consists of positing statements [*Sätze*] or systems of statements and systematically reviewing them" (1935, p. 1). Generalizing statements are not one more kind of statement within academic writing, but serve as the foundation of the research process itself.

In the results section (Section 3), we will move to an assessment of the relations between generalizing statements and the particular observations upon which they are founded. It is there that we will explore Berkeley's second criteria of generalization and the problems surrounding example-based research when it comes to the practice of generalization. All statements used in these sections have been anonymized to emphasize that our aim is not to call out any particular individuals but to illustrate a more general practice, the generality of which we will explore using the practice of predictive modeling.

For our team, generalizing statements can have two overarching forms, which we call "categorical" and "exemplary." The first, categorical, is a statement where a category or class is defined or explained. Here both the subject and verb of the statement play a role in our ability to identify it as a generalization. Consider the following four sentences, one of which we identify as not a generalization according to our schema.

Categorical Generalizations
1. While liberalism embraces the widespread dissemination of information as a democratizing force, there are those who use that information in ways that threaten the liberal ideal.
2. The entire society had been predicated on a belief that both sexes were entitled to distinct rights and responsibilities.
3. After decades in which literary study has been dominated by contextual hermeneutics, it seems possible once again to think about literary change in formal terms.
4. In this as in many other respects, royal servitors followed the example set by the court, which hired immigrants trained in "natural philosophy" (including astrology) to staff Russia's top medical and educational institutions.

In all four examples, we see how the subject of either a subordinate or main clause is a general category and not an individual instance: *liberalism, the entire society, literary study, royal servitors*. These can be of different scales (the group of royal servitors, on the one hand, or all of society, on the other), but in each case they do not refer to individual instances (a liberal person, a single study of literature). In terms of the verb, in the first three sentences we see how the verb is used in some definitional or explanatory way: "liberalism *embraces*," "the entire society *is predicated on*," "literary studies *has been dominated by*." In the fourth example, however, the general class of "servitors" is not defined but is said to have done something: they "followed the example." This for us is not a generalization. Even though it invokes a general class, it simply describes the actions of this class rather than providing a definition of it. Thus the definitional use of language is essential to the act of generalization.

The second form a generalizing statement can take is what we call "exemplification": a single individual instance is used to *stand for* some larger class. We will return in Section 4 to talking more about exemplarity, but for now, we want to focus on this type of generalization that, while less common, is still prevalent within the literature. In this case, the subject, verb, and predicate of the generalization are all important to pay attention to.

Exemplary Generalizations

5.　Taking Baumgartner's space jump as the paradigmatic form of the aesthetic, this essay outlines its salient features.

6.　In the following pages I argue that the unspoken conflict marking Exner's discussion of the compound eye may be considered a window into the way Western scientific thought has constructed a framework for vision since at least the beginning of the seventeenth century.

7.　Cavendish is relevant here, in particular, because her writing challenged the Royal Society's vision of "Real Knowledge" in ways that illustrate the importance of Restoration-era epistemology for the epistemological questions raised by anthropomorphism and the Anthropocene today.

In each case we see how something specific (the space jump, Sigmund Exner, Margaret Cavendish) is used as an example of something general (the aesthetic, Western scientific thought, Restoration-era epistemology). Indeed, in statement 7, we see how this process of exemplification is enchained in ever larger generalities: Margaret Cavendish is an exemplar of Restoration-era epistemology that is an exemplar for epistemological questions raised by the Anthropocene. And in each case, the verb or predicate that links particular and general plays a role in establishing the generality of the example: the space jump is said to be "the paradigmatic form" of the aesthetic; Exner's treatise is "a window into" Western scientific thought; Cavendish's writing "illustrates" the importance of Restoration-era epistemology.

Sometimes this exemplarity can be generative or genealogical, meaning it begins either a historical process or a thinking process. For example:

8.　The Latourian theory of hybrids provides a useful starting point for thinking about a field of inquiry in which interpretive claims are supported by evidence obtained via the exhaustive, enumerative resources of computing.

Here we see how Latour's theory is a "starting point" for "thinking about" something considerably larger in scale (in this case, an entire "field of inquiry"). Latour isn't an example of this field, but he is the framework through which subsequent generalizations about the field will be made. This can also take the form of a posited argument rather than a statement of what is:

9.　I contend that Wiener's theories have important implications for the work of modernist scholarship: his concepts of cybernetic feedback loops and mechanical learning enable a new understanding of modernists' intense preoccupation with information culture.

Here Wiener's theories "enable" a new understanding of something categorical, in this case "modernists' preoccupation with information culture." Wiener is the example that facilitates a generalization, a fact however that is stated as a contention and not self-evident ("I contend that").

One can see how the removal of the "I contend" in this sentence essentially leaves the generalizing structure of the statement intact. We will see numerous instances of such "I argue that" phrases in generalizing statements. The important point is that these phrases are implicit to all generalizations. One could insert "I contend" into any generalizing statement to foreground the probabilistic nature of the inductive statement, just as one could remove it from all statements without changing the sense of the statement. Later in in Section 4, we will return to its potential value, but for now we want to indicate that it has no effect on the grammatical structure of generalizing statements.

There are phrases, however, that do compromise the statement's identity as a generalization. The primary types that we will be conditioning on are conditional forms, principally through the verb "may" or "might." For example:

10. Accordingly, my research shows that contact may reduce whites' negative feelings toward Natives without altering whites' superior sense of group position.

This example highlights the difficulty of deciding whether or not this statement is a generalization. Technically speaking, the author has not said that contact *does* reduce negative feelings, but that it *may*. On the other hand, it is positing a general relationship that exceeds individual instances (contact between these two people at this point in time). It uses probabilistic language for what is always a probabilistic judgment about moving from instances to classes. Similar to "I argue that," one could insert "may" into every generalizing sentence without altering the underlying epistemological conditions of the sentence. To return to Karl Popper, because we can never know for certain – because a generalized theory can never be verified for all conditions and all examples for all time – in inductive scenarios, we are always operating on the premise that something *may* be true (and thus may also not be true). As discussed in the next sub-section, we will be coding these sentences as generalizations but mark them with a special attribute so that we can also observe what happens if we remove them from our data.

Another challenging example is the use of qualifiers like "some" and "many." For example:

11. Although some might view the workplace as a promising venue for reducing prejudice, this seems unlikely, as many workplaces today do not meet Allport's conditions for contact.
12. According to some models, contact may reduce prejudice because it personalizes "the other" or facilitates recognition of similarities and development of a common superordinate identity.

Saying that "some" people view the workplace as a promising venue for reducing prejudice is not to say that it actually is or even to specify in how many instances this is likely to be the case. The lack of specification makes it hard to treat this as a generalization, although for sure it is generalizing about "some" people. Similarly in the second example, we have a generalizing statement about "some models." In other words, the generalization holds true in a few cases. Is that a generalization? Even "many" poses a challenge because we do not know the scope or regularity of "many." Many workplaces do not meet certain conditions – is that a generalization or not? For the purposes of this Element, we have elected to err on the side of caution and not label these as generalizations. Only in instances where we see language like "in most cases" or "in a majority of cases" do we label something a generalization. Terms like "always," "every," and "anyone" also positively indicate a generalization, as in this example:

13. One of the things that anyone involved in the murky business of humanities scholarship comes to know, without knowing how, or perhaps without even knowing that they know it, is the difference between criticism and critique.

Here we have an example of something being true for every humanist even though they do not potentially know that it is true.

Another limiting condition is the way generalizations can be attributed to other people in a statement. We call these vicarious or "indirect" generalizations, because they allow authors and readers to indulge in generalizations but absolve themselves of the responsibility of their utterance. Indirect generalizations are an important dimension of complexity reduction for scholarship because they do not require that all statements be verified in the space of a single article but can be attributed elsewhere. Like all generalizations, they are convenient but also risky because they explicitly draw attention to the absence of evidence. For example:

14. As Bobo suggests, education remained firmly entrenched in the contemporary imagination as the nation's best path out of poverty.
15. It is thus in this very different and more productive sense that photography, for Peirce, still qualifies as an objective form of representation.
16. With relatively few exceptions, previous organizational research assumes that, when categorical systems are agreed upon, audiences are homogeneously averse to novel combinations.

In each of these cases, a generalization is posited, but the speaker of the generalization is not the author. In the first two cases, the generalization is a specific author (Bobo, Peirce); in the last example, we have a summary of existing research. The author speaks for a collective of other authors who do the generalizing. One of the questions we will be asking is the extent to which different fields use this mode of indirect generalization more often as well as the consequences of doing so.

As we have tried to show here, generalization is something that is at once linguistically legible at the statement level – it has certain criteria or qualities – and is also ambiguous. The criteria for its identification are not as rudimentary as saying "always includes verb X" or "always includes grammatical pattern Y." It depends on real-world knowledge of the generality of the terms being used with respect to some context and the definitional certainty that links subject and predicate. Our assumption is that we could never identify enough instances to encompass all possible forms of generalization, but that we may be able to identify enough to predict their presence with some degree of accuracy, where accuracy here means "others would agree with this definition."

Selecting Data

Once we have our understanding of the problem established, we then move to the selection of data to be studied. Because we want to understand how the practice of generalization works in the field of literary studies – and because we assume we cannot study every single article ever written in the field (let alone where exactly the boundaries of the "field" are) – we need a procedure to sample from this larger population such that our sample is in some way representative of that population.

To do so, we follow the sampling procedure used by the Open Science Collaboration in their reproducibility project, where they focused on a synchronic slice of articles drawn from a single year and geographic region within a subset of three "leading" journals in their field (Open Science Collaboration 2015). In our case, we select six journals from the year 2016 encompassing 151 articles (see Table 1 for a summary). Because we are interested in contextualizing this data relative to other fields, we also select another three journals, two from history and one from sociology from the same year. History was chosen as an adjacent field to literary studies due to the strong historical orientation of literary studies (Hayot 2016) as well as methodological overlap. Both of these disciplines are still predominantly qualitative in nature. We include sociology as a discipline because it arguably is the most theoretically adjacent discipline to literary studies within the social sciences, but one that is predominantly quantitative in nature. Thus we can gain some insights into the relative nature of the practice of generalization when compared to other low- and high-quantitative disciplines.

We address "leading" journals by taking the North American flagship journal for that field's primary society (*PMLA* in literary studies, the *American Sociological Review* in sociology, and the *American Historical Review* (AHR) in history, which

Table 1 Summary of journals

Journal Name	Code	Field	# Articles	Avg. Length
American Historical Review	AHR	HIST	17	9755
Journal of Modern History	JMH	HIST	15	10581
Modernism/Modernity	MM	LIT_FS	31	8478
Studies in the Novel	SN	LIT_FS	23	8221
Studies in Romanticism	SR	LIT_FS	20	7869
Critical Inquiry	CI	LIT_GEN	27	9153
New Literary History	NLH	LIT_GEN	27	8201
PMLA	PMLA	LIT_GEN	23	7769
American Sociology Review	ASR	SOC	47	9349
All			**230**	**8820**

we supplement with the *Journal in Modern History* due to the relatively low number of articles in AHR). For the remaining journals, because we have no measures of qualitative hierarchy in our field – nor is there consensus on the reliability of such measures – we choose journals based on our own beliefs of these journal's perceived quality. These are not the "best" journals (whatever that would mean) but should reasonably be taken to be "high quality" in their respective fields. Finally, in our literary studies sample we further stratify our selection of journals into two subcategories, which we denote as "general" and "field specific." We hypothesize that journals with different subdisciplinary missions may behave differently with respect to the practice of generalization. Thus, in addition to *PMLA* we choose *Critical Inquiry* and *New Literary History* as part of our "general" category and for our field-specific subset we choose two journals with a period-focused mission (*Studies in Romanticism*, *Modernism/Modernity*) and one journal with a genre-focused mission (*Studies in the Novel*).

Since the process of sampling is so important to the generalizability of any findings, we want to spend a moment reflecting on each of the criteria guiding our selection and how they might impact our interpretation of our results. First, as with the OSC project, we do not consider a true probability sample possible. A "probability sample" refers to the process of sampling whereby every unit that belongs to the population has an equal probability of being sampled. The conditions of probability sampling are that one knows the entire population being sampled along with the distribution of underlying factors in its composition (like demographic identities derived from census tabulations). The set of "literary studies journals" is arguably not fixed, with a range of boundary cases and the absence of a true index of "all" journals in the field. Thus, we do not believe that probability sampling is possible when it comes to disciplinary self-assessment because the nature of disciplinary boundaries is not highly delimited. Any sample of disciplinary units will thus not be truly random and will require further investigation regarding potential bias or skew with respect to underlying factors within the field.

Second, the logic of conditioning on leading or high-quality journals is to focus our attention on more visible academic practices. As with the OSC, our belief is that if our problem is present among top journals, then it means it is a problem worth tackling even if it is exhibited with lower levels elsewhere. By conditioning on so-called higher-quality journals, we leave open the question as to whether there is a relationship between generalization and perceived journal quality or prestige, which our project cannot immediately address. This is the subject of future research.

Third, by conditioning on journal articles, we leave out research that is published in books, whether monographs or edited volumes. While future research will want to test this relationship, our assumption is that given the greater thematic scope of books, we should see similar or even potentially higher levels of generalization in them.

Finally, by sampling from a single year, our research cannot speak to the changing nature of this practice. Nevertheless, we do provide diachronic data drawn from the JSTOR for research service on potentially related semantic behavior over time, thus providing some historical context for these practices. We also cannot assume that all articles were produced within the exact same time frame, as the pace of academic production and publication differs greatly. Nevertheless, we assume that the nature of our problem is not subject to short time spans of variation (less than five years) and that we should not expect significant variations either immediately before or after our selected year. We also do not have reason to believe that 2016 represents an anomalous year in academic publication.

As can be seen by this list, given our sampling procedure there is much that we cannot know about the practice of generalization in the field of literary studies. But the important point is not that such limitations a priori invalidate whatever findings we present here (just as sampling by itself does not a priori make one's findings valid), but that we consider the generalizability of our findings with respect to these explicit limitations. Given the degree of error with respect to our predictions and given the degree of variance with respect to our findings across our data, how reasonable is it to assume the continuity of this practice beyond the actual works sampled? Ultimately, this is why reproducibility was identified by the OSC as the single most important scholarly research practice – rather than relying on either assumptions built into any given sample as to its out-of-sample validity or assumptions of hypothetical, and untested, alternative samples, the best way to gain confidence about a problem is to continue to test it over and over again under varying conditions.

To prepare the data for annotation, all articles were manually downloaded and cleaned by hand. Cleaning included removing all headers, page numbers, and references as well as in the case of *PMLA* correcting OCR errors based on the conversion from PDFs. All other articles were downloaded as text files.

Annotating Data

Because our primary method of analysis is the use of machine learning to predict the presence of generalization within our sample, our next step is to annotate the data that will then be used to train our predictive model. Because we cannot annotate all of our data – a problem common to most machine learning exercises without pre-annotated data – we once again need a sampling method to select some of our data for annotation. The first step is to identify the unit for annotation, which following our earlier discussion, we define as the "sentence." Our primary research question relates to the prevalence and nature of generalizing statements within literary studies research and thus the sentence is for us the primary unit of analysis.

However, following existing research in the field, for the purposes of our sampling procedure we assume that not all sentences in academic articles are alike (Degaetano-Ortlieb & Teich 2017). As Degaetano-Ortlieb and Teich (2017) have shown, the linguistic behavior of sentences differs according to the location of sentences within an article (i.e., the nature of statements in an introduction differs from that in the body of an article that differs from that in the conclusion). Rather than sample randomly from entire articles, we thus choose to condition on the introduction and concluding sections because we assume that this is where the practice of generalization is more likely to occur. Profiling these sections allows us to condition on areas where our activity of interest is more robust and representative and thus will provide a better representation of the practice for our algorithmic (and human) learning process. We therefore randomly sample an equal number of sentences (N=30) from every article conditioning on the first 1,500 words and final 1,000 words of an article. Because articles in literary studies and history do not uniformly indicate section headers, we use conservative word length proxies for consistency.

Next, to guide our annotation process, we created the following annotation scheme based on our collective readings and discussions. Per our previous discussion, sentences could be given one of three labels:

a. neutral

b. generalization

c. exemplification

The linguistic features discussed above are used to identify the presence of a generalization. For example, sentence 2 would be considered a generalization:

2. The entire society had been predicated on a belief that both sexes were entitled to distinct rights and responsibilities.

An exemplification is a special instance of when a particular example was expressly stated as being representative of some general population, as in sentence 5:

5. Taking Baumgartner's space jump as the paradigmatic form of the aesthetic, this essay outlines its salient features.

We also added two conditional categories associated with generalization:

b.1 attributed

b.2 conditional

"Attributed" refers to cases of generalization that were attributed to a speaker other than the article author, as in sentence 14:

14. As Bobo suggests, education remained firmly entrenched in the contemporary imagination as the nation's best path out of poverty.

"Conditional" refers to cases that use delimiting words such as "may" or "might":

10. Accordingly, my research shows that contact may reduce whites' negative feelings toward Natives without altering whites' superior sense of group position.

Finally, we decided that we would use a binary labeling scheme of 0/1 to indicate generalization rather than a weighted scheme to indicate confidence (that a sentence was more or less likely to be a generalization). Based on our readings and discussion, our team believed that generalization was not a matter of degree, but of kind. Future research will want to experiment with other potential annotation schemes and explore the effect that weighted annotations have on modeling and prediction.

Because the annotation task was considerable in scope and also, as we will show, conceptually challenging, we decided as a group that the final annotated set would be undertaken by a single domain expert, in this case myself, the author of this Element. Crucial to this decision was that we would validate the extent to which my annotations agreed with other team members' annotations, a necessary step in any annotation process. Future work will want to explore the efficacy of domain-expert annotation versus more general layperson annotations undertaken by greater numbers of people when it comes to annotating complex textual phenomena (Gius, Reiter, & Willand 2019).

To develop our shared understanding of the problem, we undertook several rounds of informal (unmeasured) annotation, followed by discussion of our results. Seeing where we agreed or disagreed helped formalize our notion of what a generalization was. We then developed a codebook to give annotators a shared basis for annotation, which we provide in the supplemental data and that is also recapitulated here.

To assess our agreement, we used a sample of 116 sentences drawn from articles not included in our final sample, which were annotated by four readers listed earlier, two undergraduates, one faculty member from another discipline, and myself. Since I would be the eventual annotator, we then measured the extent to which my annotations agreed with the majority vote of the other three annotators. We wanted to measure what the likelihood was that I could reproduce the consensus judgments of others. In essence, we treated my work like a predictive model and measured my predictions against some "ground truth." The advantage of this is it allows us to compare the degree of variability of the primary human annotator relative to other humans with the algorithmic classifications relative to the human annotator, creating a spectrum of human-machine judgment.

Table 2 provides an overview of these levels of agreement. (The underlying annotations are included in the supplementary data.) While we will go into more detail regarding the algorithmic classification below, it is worth pausing here to reflect on the high levels of disagreement at the human level. We might understand and address this in several ways. The first is that we assume that the notion of generalization is *intrinsically* ambiguous. We expect that no amount of training or discussion will allow us to arrive at universal agreement. Rather than see this as a flaw, we see it as an affordance of machine learning

Table 2 F1 scores for correctly predicting generalizing sentences
The human classifier was measured against a group of three other human readers while the machine classifier was measured against the primary human annotator.

	Human (N=116)	Machine (N=3456)
Accuracy	0.664	0.745
Sensitivity (True Positive Rate)	0.691	0.837
Specificity (True Negative Rate)	0.649	0.648

because it allows us to learn "representations" of complex ideas and study their behavior as well as their construction. We can engage with the process of how the concept of "generalization" is constructed and thus see it as something perspectival in nature. The notion of "ground truth" that circulates within machine learning communities is more misleading than useful and should always be thought of as a construction of some sort.

The intrinsic ambiguity of our category notwithstanding, I think future work might want to explore several directions to mitigate ambiguity when applying machine learning to complex linguistic phenomena. The first is to question our decision to include nonexperts and non-domain-experts in the annotation process. Generalization is a highly complex and potentially discipline-specific practice. Our initial idea of trying to arrive at an understanding that was more "general" may have led to higher levels of perceived ambiguity than there really are. Had we trained only experts in literary studies, my assumption is we would have arrived at higher levels of inter-rater agreement.

Second, we could have spent more time training. While we did engage in weeks of discussion and three rounds of practice, we definitely could have spent longer to align our understanding. There is a certain arbitrariness about when one stops to "test" agreement. The risk here is the same as for machine learning – the risk of overfitting so that while "we" might all agree with one another after some amount of time, our understanding would not generalize well to others. Continuing to test agreement until it is high only tells us that these readers were able to learn this problem, but it does not mean it will be universally shared.

Finally, it is possible that our annotation process, whereby readers were only given individual sentences without knowledge of context, might have hampered their ability to achieve agreement, especially for nonexperts. Seeing sentences within context might have increased levels of agreement about any individual sentence's generalizing aims.

Overall, the main point to take away, however, is that ambiguity is not something we want to do away with but need to incorporate into our analysis. We can use a variety of techniques to adjust and qualify our estimates to accommodate this uncertainty. Uncertainty is part of the research process and acknowledging and quantifying this uncertainty is one of the core features that distinguishes computational research from more traditional forms of analysis.

Implementation and Validation

After assessing levels of reader agreement, I then moved on to annotating sentences, for a total of 3,456 sentences sampled according to the criteria listed earlier, with a minimum of 14 sentences annotated per article and a maximum of

22. It is important to emphasize that this process took a considerable amount of time (and concentration to focus on so many examples!). These annotations were then used to build a predictive model of generalizing sentences. Generalizations and exemplifications were collapsed into a single category making it a binary classification process due to the sparsity of exemplifcations.

Sunyam Bagga undertook the process of predictive modeling using the annotated sentences as training data. He explored a variety of deep learning models using pre-trained GloVe and ELMo embeddings, which have proven the most successful on sentence-level prediction tasks because they take into account large amounts of contextual data and do not only rely on existing word counts (Peters et al. 2018, Devlin et al. 2019). As can be seen in Table 3, using a process of 3-fold cross validation, the best performing model was a CNN using ELMo embeddings (f1 = 0.769). Although we do not show it here, we can report that these results were about 10 percentage points better than more traditional classification models like logistic regression or SVMs. The best performing model was then used to predict sentences across the entire sample, once again conditioning on the first 1,500 words and concluding 1,000 words of articles from which we only keep full sentences (N=16,816).

To give readers a sense of the range and reliability of the predictions, we provide examples of correctly and incorrectly classified sentences according to different levels of confidence (low = close to 0.5, high = greater than 0.99). For every prediction in the training data, we produce both a binary

Table 3 Various classification models employed with reported accuracy scores in descending order of performance

Model	F1-score	Precision	Recall	Accuracy	AUPRC
cnn + ELMo	0.769	0.713	0.837	0.745	0.830
bilstm + ELMo	0.757	0.724	0.795	0.741	0.795
stacked bilstm + ELMo	0.750	0.707	0.800	0.729	0.795
lstm + ELMo	0.742	0.708	0.780	0.724	0.789
bert	0.736	0.672	0.814	0.703	0.776
cnn (GloVe)	0.696	0.709	0.688	0.696	0.756
stacked bilstm (GloVe)	0.665	0.687	0.650	0.669	0.708
lstm (GloVe)	0.595	0.691	0.540	0.641	0.697
bilstm (GloVe)	0.591	0.696	0.524	0.638	0.688

classification and the probability of the classification. These scores can be used in future research to explore different thresholds of selection (potentially only considering generalizations with higher likelihood) and their impact on subsequent results. As can be seen with the false positives, low-confidence false positives are deeply ambiguous sentences with respect to their generality, while the high-confidence false positives often appear to be simply falsely annotated (i.e., mislabeled). In other words, when the algorithm is confident and wrong, it may point to the annotator being wrong. Future work might wish to explore "updating" annotations through a process of iterative learning, which may be important for projects that address highly ambiguous underlying material.

True Positives
[Correctly identified generalizations]
17. (High confidence) Ontological concerns like these have structured thought about copyright since the beginnings of the Romantic period.
18. (Low confidence) Sometimes we're clearly identifying our bodies with the kinetic activity in front of us, sometimes it's as if we feel it impinging on us, and sometimes it's a fuzzy amalgam of the two.

True Negatives
[Correctly identified non-generalizations]
19. (High confidence) This year, the Hebrew writer Ruby Namdar was awarded the Sapir Prize for Hebrew literature for his novel *HaBayit Asher Nekhrav* (The Ruined House), making him the first recipient of the award who was not a resident of Israel.
20. (Low confidence) Similarly, when he is obliged to debate western geography with the owner of the Alta Loma hotel, who insists that Boulder is in Nebraska rather than Colorado, we see that Bandini has a more intimate awareness of the makeup of the western United States than many others do.

False Positives
[Non-generalizations that were identified as generalizations]
21. (Low confidence) Much of what is published in the latter is lost, given how few people collect them, and it would be beneficent to gather the different volumes of such periodicals and cut out articles on science.
22. (High confidence) In other words, the vauntingly impotent humanities may earn a slice of power if they give up a large measure of their presumptuous dominion over the realm of "the human."

False Negatives
[Generalizations that were identified as non-generalizations]
23. (Low confidence) In this sense, Colombia is a "crucial case" for evaluating the hypothesis that internal wars can promote state building under certain specific circumstances.

24. (High confidence) After thirtysome years of impressive mileage and increasing returns milked from the ANT farm, Latour attempted to relocate his operations on a slightly different, more discriminating, plane.

In the next section, we provide a semantic review of the model to better understand the more general semantic orientations of what it has learned, which cannot be inferred from individual examples alone.

3 Results

The Prevalence of Generalization

After all of these steps – theorizing our problem; collecting, cleaning, and annotating our data; and finally validating our model – we can move on to an analysis of results. It cannot be emphasized enough that the transparency associated with computational modeling and the steps required to assess the generalizability of one's model lead to an enormous amount of mediating labor. Each of these steps also represents its own avenues for further research.

In this section, we present results regarding the distribution of generalization across our data. In particular, we explore levels across fields, journals, and researcher types (with respect to gender, rank, and institutional prestige). To account for known ambiguity in our prediction process, we use two primary techniques to incorporate the estimated amount of error (or uncertainty) with respect to sentence-level annotations in our analysis: first, we implement a bootstrap sampling method to estimate the sample mean of generalizing sentences for each field and journal. This gives us an idea of the variance of generalization within our sample and subsamples. Second, we implement a modification of our observed levels of generalization using Rogan and Gladen's (1978) approach to estimating the true prevalence of a phenomenon given known errors in its detection. This approach adjusts the actual prevalence in a given sample according to the sample size and amount of error in the specificity and sensitivity of the predictions. It is often used in epidemiology to estimate the true prevalence of a disease given known screening errors. In other words, given that there is a known degree of error in identifying a disease (in this case, generalization), how does this error affect our estimation of the amount of the disease in our sample?

Comparing our three fields, we see that there is a statistically significant difference in the estimated mean rate for literary studies when compared to history and sociology (Figure 1). An analysis of variance shows that the effect of field was significant on the rate of generalization ($F(2,2997) = 11,162$, $p < 2e-16$). While the estimated mean rates for sociology and history were surprisingly similar at 54.4% (+/− 0.8%) and 53.8% (+/− 1.0%) respectively, the estimated rate for literary

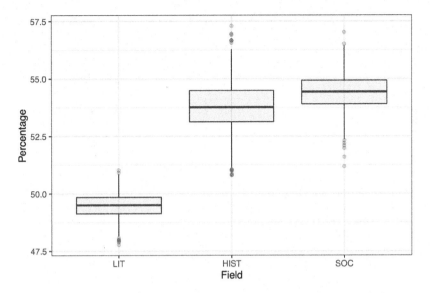

Figure 1 Estimated percentage of generalizing sentences across different fields based on 1,000 bootstrapped samples per field (N=16,816)

studies is just less than five percentage points lower at 49.5% (+/− 0.5%). Nevertheless, according to our model, articles in literary studies are generalizing one out of an estimated every two sentences within their introductions and conclusions, only a slightly lower amount than a highly quantitative field like sociology.

Using Rogan and Gladen's method to estimate the true prevalence of generalization given known detection error, we find that the estimated prevalence of generalizing sentences drops significantly due to the high degree of ambiguity in the prediction process. For history and sociology, we expect the true rate of generalization to be closer to 38%–39% of sentences and for literary studies close to 30%. Thus a conservative estimate would place the practice for literary studies closer to one-third of all introductory and concluding sentences of an article. If we take all of this information together, we can safely conclude that generalization is a *regular* practice within the framing of research in literary studies and that while not identical to rates in highly quantified fields like sociology, it occurs at comparable levels.

When we turn to journal-specific analysis, we see some interesting results with respect to the differential rates of generalization across different fields (Figure 2). Certain journals in literary studies, like *Critical Inquiry* and *New Literary History*, have rates of generalization on par with sociology, while the field-specific journals all have lower than average rates, relative to the overall

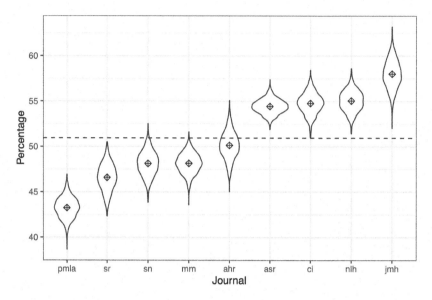

Figure 2 Estimated percentage of generalizing sentences across different journals based on 1,000 bootstrapped samples per journal (N=16,816)

sample mean. While *PMLA* is considered to be a "general" literary studies journal in our sample, it evidences the lowest levels of generalization overall, a full 10 percentage points lower than a journal like *Critical Inquiry*, suggesting that its mission is crucially different from that of these other "general" journals. What this works out to in practice is that one can expect to see roughly nine to ten more generalizing statements in the opening of an article in *Critical Inquiry* when compared to one in *PMLA*. The *Journal of Modern History* tops our list with rates of generalization close to 60%, significantly higher than even sociology. Overall, these results suggest that there are important differences between journals, but that these differences do not drastically affect the overall rates we are seeing by field. We thus expect that expanded or different samples would behave similarly at the overall field level, with anticipated smaller differences to be shown at the journal level.

If we condition only on exemplification as a special kind of generalization, we see a reverse effect. Here we use the hand-annotated data because the sparsity of annotations was not sufficient to build a classifier. Based on our sample, we see how sociology almost never uses this form of generalization, while the field-specific journals in literary studies engage in considerably higher practices, though general literary studies journals are not far behind (Table 4). The largely quantitative field of sociology almost never suggests that a single item stands for some larger whole, but neither does the field of history in most

Table 4 Percentage of exemplary
generalizations by field using the
hand-annotated data

Field	Exemplification
SOC	0.3%
HIST	2.8%
LIT_GEN	7.1%
LIT_FS	9.9%

Table 5 Output of linear regression estimating percentage of
generalizing statements per article based on different researcher
identities

	Estimate	Std. Error	t value	Pr(>|t|)
(Intercept)	0.52653	0.01753	30.041	<2e-16
genderW	−0.02867	0.01735	−1.652	0.0996
rankAssoc	−0.01851	0.02514	−0.736	0.462
rankFull	−0.01233	0.02193	−0.562	0.5745
rankNT	0.03616	0.02362	1.531	0.1269
ivy_plus	0.02484	0.02163	1.148	0.2517

cases. It seems that exemplification is a specifically literary phenomena, one that increases in strength the more particular the research.

One of the questions we also want to ask is whether different kinds of researchers use generalization at differing rates. While we see interesting differences across fields and journals, do we also see differences at the level of individual researcher types? Is it the case that more senior researchers, or researchers at more prestigious institutions, or researchers who identify with a particular gender are more likely to make generalizing statements than the population as a whole? To test this, we use multiple linear regression with our dependent variable as the percentage of generalizing sentences per article and independent dummy variables for gender, rank, and institutional prestige. We define institutional prestige as belonging to an "ivy+" group, which includes a small set of schools in addition to Ivy League schools. Across all of our categories, we see no significant predictors of rates of generalization $(F(5,288) = 1.967, p = 0.0836, R^2 = 0.033)$ (Table 5). While gender approaches significance, the average rate of decrease (< 3%) seems insignificant from a real-world perspective.

The Semantics of Generalization

Estimating the extent of generalization within literary research provides us with one way of understanding the issue. Knowing more about the qualities of such generalizations can also help us better understand the problem. In this section, we turn to an analysis of semantic indicators of generalization, with a particular emphasis on questions of time. When articles invoke temporal frameworks, what are the most frequent scales at which they do so? At what temporal scales are researchers working and how do they compare with those in disciplines like history and sociology?

For the data in this section, we begin by analyzing the distinctive words of generalizing sentences compared with sentences that were predicted not to entail generalizations within the field of literary studies (Table 6). For this analysis, we both consider articles in full and provide some historical data to situate these practices within the recent history of the discipline (dating back to 1950). What are the historical trends surrounding such potential indicators of generalization?

As we can see from Table 6, when scholars make generalizations they are significantly more likely to invoke concepts related to time, culture, literature,

Table 6 List of the 15 most distinctive words of generalizing sentences as measured by Dunning's log-likelihood ratio
Raw counts in each class are included.

Term	Count (Gen)	Count (Non)	LLR
literary	476	105	103.6
century	203	21	92.0
human	366	79	82.1
culture	189	32	57.1
humanities	141	18	55.1
cultural	213	43	52.3
modern	208	42	51.1
modernism	120	16	45.3
social	257	67	42.2
aesthetic	192	42	42.2
scientific	106	16	35.9
cognitive	105	16	35.2
understanding	105	16	35.2
history	270	79	34.9
scholars	86	11	33.5

history, modernity, humanity, as well as other scholars. While this list should not surprise us, it gives us confidence that the model has indeed learned the concepts and categories around which scholars in literary studies tend to generalize most often. Indeed, it would be hard to imagine how one might "particularize" about categories like the "human" or the "humanities." This list also begs the question of how example-based scholarship – providing one or a few examples of something – could ever be sufficient to ground a generalization about "culture" or "modernity." As I will show in the next sub-section, generalizations can take many different forms and flavors. They need not only be about such massively large abstractions. But in each instance, I will try to indicate the extent to which example-based research comes up dramatically short when it comes to providing evidence to ground the generalizations that circulate within the field.

The list in Table 6 indicates that at least some of the generalizing impulse in literary studies relates to the category of time. To test this further, and to provide some points of comparison, we look at the full text of articles in our data set and condition on a small set of temporally oriented language. What we see when we do so (Figure 3) is how the predominant temporal foci of each field differ in telling ways: literary studies focuses principally on the "modern," even with the modernism journal removed, while history's primary concern is the "century." Sociology by contrast focuses very little on these large-scale abstractions and focuses instead more on the "year." While it may appear from the word cloud that literary studies has an overall stronger orientation around time, this is due to the larger sample set used when compared to the other disciplines. History actually has a larger portion of its vocabulary explicitly focused on the language of time than literary studies (which of course makes sense as a discipline fundamentally organized around time).

Figure 3 Word clouds of temporal words by field sized by frequency of occurrence. From top to bottom: literary studies, history, sociology.

Figure 3 (cont.)

Figure 3 (cont.)

One question that emerged from this initial analysis was how the relationship of different temporal scales plays out in different fields and between fields. For example, we know that "periodization" is a strong factor organizing literary studies (Underwood 2016). But what is the relationship between a rhetorical emphasis on periods and smaller time scales, like a year, or a year to even smaller scales like a day? How do these frameworks relate to one another?

Measuring time is an intrinsically difficult challenge when it comes to discourse (Piper & Sachs 2018). Our efforts here can only begin to scratch the surface of understanding the temporal frameworks of research in literary studies. Our measures are designed to function as potential indicators of temporal attention, with the hope that future work will elaborate more fully on these trends. As we will see, the trends revealed here are so severe that our estimation is that they will likely remain resistant to any underlying ambiguity in the data. Even this initial rudimentary understanding reveals important insights about discursive practices that are prevalent within the field.

To measure periods, we construct a small set of designations common to the field (such as "classical," "baroque," "medieval," "Victorian") as well as more general terms that capture large time frames (such as "past," "present," and "future"). (The full list appears in the supplementary data.) To measure the idea of the "year," we look at both explicit invocations of the term "year(s)," as well as four-digit strings that do not appear in parentheses (i.e., are not used as references) and encompass current human history (i.e., range from 1000 to 2020 and also may contain an "s" as in "1960s"). For the scale of the day, we measure the explicit invocation of the term "day(s)," names of days of the week, and a small set of words associated with daily time frames ("afternoon," "clock," "hour," "minute," etc.).

As we can see from Table 7, both history and sociology refer to years far more often than large-scale periods (46%–68% more often), while literary studies refers to large-scale periods *three times more often* than it tends to reference a given year or decade.

At the same time, we can also see how this trend is reversed when we look at the smaller scale of the "day." In this case, as shown in Table 8, literary studies is 37% more likely to refer to a time frame related to the span of a single day than it is to an entire year, while history and sociology are 3–3.5x more likely to refer to years than days. In other words, what we are seeing is interesting evidence to suggest that literary studies has a bifocal temporal perspective that is worth

Table 7 Ratio and counts of year and period references across fields

Field	Year (Count)	Period (Count)	Ratio
LIT	721	2225	0.32
HIST	486	332	1.46
SOC	830	494	1.68

Table 8 Ratio and counts of day and year references across fields

Field	Day (Count)	Year (Count)	Ratio
LIT	989	721	1.37
HIST	141	486	0.29
SOC	285	830	0.34

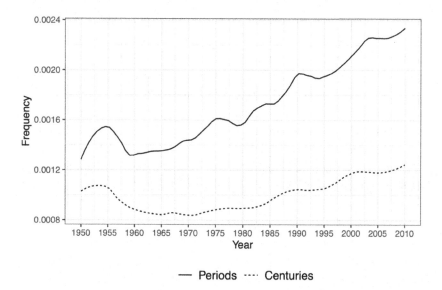

Figure 4 Yearly frequency of large-scale time-related words in academic articles within literary studies, 1950–2010 (N=63,397)

further investigating, as researchers appear to shift between very small time scales to very large ones. Such heterochrony is worth further reflection, both to its actual prevalence as well as its function.

Finally, we look at the extent to which these categories have changed focus over the past half-century. To do so, we draw on a data set consisting of 63,397 articles from 60 journals in the field of literary studies published between 1950 and 2010 drawn from the JSTOR Data for Research platform (also provided in the supplementary data). Here we measure the yearly rate of our period terms relative to the terms "century+centuries" to better understand the changing distribution of attention to these different time scales. As we can see in Figure 4, there has been roughly a 100% increase in the use of period terms in literary studies over the past half-century, and a 63% increase in the use of the term "century" or "centuries." The rates of use we are seeing today are the culmination of decades of increasing generalization when it comes to time scales in literary studies. Lest we think this might be a sign of specialization, that is, a reining in of other kinds of even more general generalizations, Figure 5 indicates that the range of what we might call "super-generalizations" is also increasing, with a particular emphasis on things *social* and *literary*. We are generalizing more and more about historical epochs as well as transhistorical categories like social and literary phenomena.

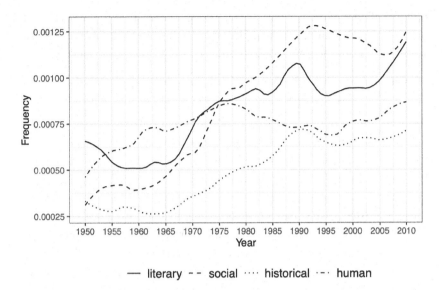

— literary - - social ···· historical ·- · human

Figure 5 Yearly frequency of terms in academic articles within literary studies, 1950–2010 (N=63,397). Source: JSTOR Data for Research.

On Evidentiary Holes

Skeptical readers might at this point be asking themselves the classic, "so what?" question. Let's assume for a moment that the rates and scale of generalization we are reporting are roughly accurate. What if they are sufficiently justified by the evidence presented in the bodies of the articles? After all, as Berkeley argued, generalization consists of both a rhetorical dimension (the linguistic dimensions of the statement itself) and an evidentiary dimension (the way particular observations are elicited to inform the generalization). Generalization is as much procedural as it is rhetorical.

In this section, I want to do a deeper dive into examples of generalization in literary scholarship to illustrate the kinds of evidentiary lacunae that they introduce. Close reading can be a useful tool here because of the way it can help draw attention to the evidentiary insufficiencies surrounding the practice of generalization in an example-based research environment. The "so what" here is the way these practices elicit serious issues of credibility with respect to evidentiary claims, ones that cannot be solved through the use of examples alone.

For heuristic purposes, I am going to posit three kinds of generalizations within my analysis, though others may want to propose broader or more complex taxonomies. The first is what I call *contextual generalizations*. These are statements that establish a context that is then mobilized in explanatory fashion within the article, while the context itself is never subject to scrutiny or proof. In these examples, an unproven context is selected to explain another selection at a smaller scaler. Take for example the following sentence:

25. Both Grimmelshausen and Saro-Wiwa write out of a postwar context in which a vernacular language extends across a divided regional space without the backing of a state authority.

In this example, we see how two writers are linked through the similarity of their contexts. Despite differences of time and language, writing in a "postwar context" connects them. On the surface, there appears to be little wrong with this statement. It seems plausible enough. And yet this frame is assumed, not shown – at what point is one no longer writing in a postwar context in human history? What are the boundaries of this context? The two examples are connected not only through the political context of "postwar" but also a linguistic context in which "vernacular language" is said to extend geographically without the backing of "state authority." Here again, we encounter a variety of under-specifications: what does vernacular language entail? What does it mean to extend across geographical space (how does language "move")? And what does the absence of state authority mean? These are all interesting questions in and of themselves – what is the relationship between the circulation of particular types of language in relation to particular types of political authority – but none of them is actually specified or documented in the article. Rather than prove that these two writers' postwar contexts are similar according to a variety of criteria, this similarity is assumed so that the similarity between the writers can then be proven in the body of the article. The unproven context becomes the medium through which the comparative act is motivated. Two writers are similar because we assume, but do not prove, that their contexts are similar.

Here is another example of contextual generalization:

26. This birth had been going on for a long time before modernism, and modernism is far from the only literary response to secularization, but modernism did develop distinctive techniques for representing the secular as more and other than the mere subtraction of religion from political and economic institutions or daily life.

In this example, we have a context called "modernism" that is generalized about with respect to other contexts – the whole here is defined as a part with respect to an even greater whole (in this case "secularization"). Modernism, which is here not defined, is said to be "distinctive" with respect to other periods, themselves not defined, according to criteria (here called "representing the secular") that are similarly not defined (or only defined through generalities – "more" and "other" than the subtraction of religion from "political and economic institutions or daily life"). In a mere sentence, a whole series of interacting generalities are being posited – a literary movement, two types of social institutions, daily life, and a discursive process related to human belief (religion/secularization). Rather than explore the generalization itself – how did a particular cohort of texts grouped under the label "modernism" develop "distinctive" techniques of representing secularization, and how might we define the "representation" of "the secular," ideas like "subtraction," or political or economic "institutions," not to mention "daily life" — instead, this litany of generalities is posited as an interpretive framework for something else. Modernism "did."

Here is a third and final example of the practice of contextual generalization:

27. Eighteenth-century novelists were compelled to invoke the cultural authority of other narrative genres, such as history, biography, the travelogue and the memoir, while simultaneously specifying what distinguished novelistic 'truth' from these genres.

In this sentence, we encounter a discussion of the general class of "eighteenth-century novelists." Here what is particularly interesting is the way an absent causal force "compels" this entire group to behave in a certain way (they "were compelled"). This behavior is described as an "invocation" of other genres, though what it means to "invoke" the "cultural authority" of another genre is not specified. At the same time, these writers, who are never specified in their number, range, or attributes, also "specify" a category called "novelistic 'truth,'" which is also not specified. A general group of people who are never specified are forced to engage in generalizable behavior of "specification" that is itself not specified by an invisible force that is also not specified. Within each generality resides an entire research program – defining which eighteenth-century novelists behaved in this way (more or less strongly), what were the forces that compelled them to behave in this way, what it means to "invoke" something in a text, how one would define "cultural authority," which other genres are more strongly invoked than others (or do they all behave the same?), what texts we are talking about when we speak of these genres, and finally what novelistic "truth" is and how might it be understood to be "distinguished."

What we see at work in these examples are generalizations that are based on a priori certainties, where boundaries and causes are posited but not explicated or tested. Modernism did develop; eighteenth-century novelists were compelled; a postwar context does extend. There is an inverse relationship between the scale of the claim and the specificity of its demarcation. The bigger it gets, the fuzzier it gets. In each case, the generalization is supported by the lack of specification of its parts.

The second category I will call *disciplinary generalizations*, which might be thought of as a subset of the first. This is where an author constructs a *scholarly* context that motivates their own work. Sometimes it might take the form of a sweeping statement about the field, other times through a list of pieces that are said to represent some larger whole. These statements are crucial for adjudicating the novelty of an author's claim – has this already been said before? – and for positioning the claim with respect to other claims. It is theoretically possible to write a literature review without a generalization – one can engage with individual works and never make a claim for their representativeness. But as with the previous examples, this is not what actually happens.

Take for example this statement, which I have previously cited and which appears without a footnote:

28. Over the past few decades, humanists have insisted that it is important to resist generalizations.

Here we have a sentence that rather ironically generalizes about humanists' resistance to generalization. In doing so, it invokes an under-specified time frame (how many decades?), an entire class of writers (all humanists?), and a type of speech (what does it mean to insist?). There is a kind of fairy-tale structure to this kind of statement – not only in its somewhat fantastic temporality but also in its didactic intent. The context of a generalization taboo invoked here will be used to motivate the article's argument for the importance of generalization. To be sure, examples will be marshaled to show that some humanists have indeed insisted that generalizations should be resisted. But the "some" is dropped in the attempt to generalize the claims being made. If all or most people say something it surely matters, but does it matter if some people say something? This goes to one of the root problems of the lacunae of humanist generalization – what is the value of a few things? The continual recourse to generalization suggests an implicit belief system that there is in fact not that much value. Rather than say "some," we want our evidence to be valid for "all."

We can see a similar temporal logic at work in the next example, but here rather than generalize about an entire class of scholars, the emphasis is on a trend or growth:

29. Increasingly in recent years, the issue of the common – in its various facets of the common world, the common heritage, the commons, the creative commons, and so forth – has been explored by social theorists.

The issue of the common is increasingly being explored. This feels like an innocent enough statement. Examples are provided and they seem like good examples. But we have no measurement that accompanies an overtly quantitative claim. Increasing: from what to what, by how much, how fast, is this more than other "issues"? Given the fact that the number of academic articles increases every year, potentially every issue is "increasingly explored." This is akin to saying something has been discussed and so I will discuss it.

Unproven quantitative claims like "increasingly explored" are similar to those that claim a topic's "centrality":

30. Digital search offers release from place-based research practices that have been central to our discipline's epistemology and ethics alike.

In each case, the researcher wants to make the case for a topic's relevance, which is based on a latent, but never demonstrated, argument about quantitative prevalence. Something is "increasing" or "central" and therefore warrants attention, but that increase or centrality is never actually demonstrated. Not only does the assumption of centrality foreclose what one means by centrality, it also leaves unaddressed how the practice connects to further generalities like "disciplinary epistemology" or "ethics." These claims rely on what Polanyi might have called "tacit knowledge," things that we (think we) know as practitioners such that we do not have to explicate them (Polanyi 2009). They have a strong group-formation structure to them.

For example, in this sentence we see the writer moving up the ladder of disciplinary generalization:

31. On the one hand, interpretation – the close reading of individual texts – seems to be alive and well in the work of many, if not most, writers affiliated with cognitive literary studies.

"Alive and well" is another euphemism for "centrality," reinforced by the escalating move from "many" to "most." Once again we can see writers shying away from simply saying "some" and moving toward explicitly quantifiable claims but doing so without quantifiable evidence.

In the next and final example, we can see how an assumed consensus is further assumed to have been assailed by a new consensus, which appears to be so consensual as to require no evidentiary support:

32. The hard-won poststructuralist consensus regarding the inadmissibility of any essentialist, transhistorical concept of "Man," while it may not have been simply rejected, was assailed by a concerted attack from the hard sciences and the Realpolitik of a worldwide neoliberal hegemony.

Here we have a cascade of generalizations: poststructuralist consensus, Man, the hard sciences, a worldwide neoliberal hegemony, all of them assumed, none of them put to critical reflection. What could be the purpose of these kinds of non-evidence-based statements within an academic context?

The third type of generalization is what I will call *recipient generalizations*, whereby scholars generalize about an ideal reader or recipient of textual information, which is in turn mobilized to justify a particular textual interpretation. It too is similar to the previous two types of generalization in that it provides an un- or under-specified contextual frame that then serves as the basis of interpretation. But where the other two types relied on either historical or disciplinary context, here recipient generalizations rely on the text's implied user.

In some cases, the recipient of a text is presumed to be a scholar, like the article's author:

33. We interpret texts by projecting them against an aspect of our worldview, and this "projection" constitutes the ground of a given interpretation.

Here "we" are said to do something as readers – project texts – although this type of behavior is never actually demonstrated or proven in the article. It leaves open both the interesting question as to what exactly it means to "project" a text as well as how homogenous this practice is across the group of "we" scholars. Is this what all of us do? Some of us? Many of us? Some of the time, all of the time? And what does it mean for something to be the "ground" of an interpretation? How does this work in practice and how might one test whether it does in fact occur when (some, many) scholars interpret texts (sometimes, always)?

In other cases, the imagined reader is a sort of "everyperson":

34. When letters and books become objects of bodily correspondence and identification, they emerge as the equals of the subjects who engage them, creating an ethos of animistic inclusion.

In this example, we have a generalization about the classes of "letters" and "books" as well as the "subjects who engage them." The first two generalities interact with the third to produce a fourth generalization about an "ethos of animistic inclusion." Is this true for all letters and books? How do (some types of) letters and books become objects of "bodily identification" and what does bodily identification mean? However this works, does it happen for all people all the time? Again, there is no qualification whatsoever as a model of reading is proposed whose mechanisms are totally opaque and that is assumed to be universally valid for all objects and all people for all time. Why not say explicitly, "My theory is that when …, " rather than insist that these things are true?

And finally, in this last example we can see two streams collide, as the imagined universal reader is used as a justification for a disciplinary self-defense:

35. That version of self-collected experience is, ultimately, what many defenders of the humanities want to locate on one side of the divided kingdom, perhaps on the grounds that no one sees or feels a statistical pattern.

"No one sees or feels a statistical pattern" – to leave a statement like this unreferenced and unproven is such a deep form of intellectual hubris it begs incredulity.

In my hand-annotated sample of more than 3,000 sentences, I did not find a single example where readers were invoked that was accompanied by any delimiting criteria. While there are entire fields devoted to the empirical study of actual readers' behavior, in literary studies it appears that there are only imagined readers, who then slip unseen into our discourse as a form of evidence for our claims. The imagined reader, like the imagined context, can be made to support anything.

My point in walking through these examples is to illustrate that when we have such large-scale generalizations in the context of example-based research, we will *always* (yes always) encounter not only the kinds of massive gaps on display here between what has been observed and what has been claimed. We will necessarily encounter the conceptual and logical short cuts and shorthands that we have seen because there is no mechanism through which they could be justified using exemplary cases. When we generalize at the scale and prevalence at which we do, our evidence will always appear fantastical.

Does this mean we ought to give up entirely on case-based research? No. Does it mean we ought to change how we use case-based research? Yes.

In the following section, I will make a case for what I think we need to do to address these evidentiary holes.

III Discussion

4 Don't Generalize (from Case Studies): The Case for Open Generalization

In 1805, Friedrich Schleiermacher began holding a series of lectures at the University of Halle on the concept of "hermeneutics," which he defined as "the art of correctly understanding the speech of another." He did so, he later said, in response to lectures he had begun giving on the exegesis of the New Testament. "I found it indispensable," he said, "to provide as precise an accounting as possible of the principles of my method in order to proceed cautiously in my own interpretations and to make my judgments of other interpreters both clear and sure" (Schleiermacher, 1977, p. 8). In returning to what he called "the general principles" of interpretation, Schleiermacher would repeatedly emphasize, in words that echoed the work of Lorenzo Valla several centuries earlier, the necessity of understanding the historical totality from which individual acts of speech sprung: "Every act of speech can thus only be understood through knowledge of the historical life-totality to which it belongs [*Jede Rede kann ferner nur verstanden werden durch die Kenntnis des geschichtlichen Gesamtlebens, wozu sie gehört*] (p. 77). Or one page later:

> It follows that every human is on the one hand a place in which an inherited language forms in a unique way and his speech is only to be understood within the totality of language. [*Hiernach ist jeder Mensch auf der einen Seite ein Ort, in welchem sich eine gegebene Sprache auf eine eigentümliche Weise gestaltet, und seine Rede ist nur zu verstehen aus der Totalität der Sprache.*] (p. 78)

Schleiermacher's emphasis on the "historical life-totality," as he called it, as a key to understanding documents can be seen as a direct descendent of the work of Lorenzo Valla that I discussed in Section 1. Valla's method depended on the reconstruction of a historical context to demonstrate the anachronistic nature of the papal decree's language. The growing historicization of literary studies that we saw in Section 3 is one sign of the ways in which this hermeneutic imperative, pioneered by Valla and codified by Schleiermacher, has become deeply institutionalized in the present.

And yet Schleiermacher's method was not only a personal response to the required institutionalization of biblical exegesis that accompanied his faculty position. It was also a methodological response to an inherited tradition of textual interpretation that relied, as Detlev Kopp and Nikolaus Wegmann (1988) have shown, on an all-too-close form of close reading. Schleiermacher's emphasis on "the totality of language," of seeing the linguistic forest for the trees, was a salvo at inherited exegetical methods that focused too much on analyzing single words or citations taken out of context often for imitative purposes. Through this, one lost a sense of the whole of thought, what Schleiermacher called "*die Gemeinschaftlichkeit des Denkens*" (1977, p. 76). As Johann Bergk argued in his reading guidebook, *The Art of Reading Books* [Die Kunst Bücher zu lesen] from 1797: the reader was not only supposed to "understand the meaning of individual words, but survey the whole and through this develop a sense of reflection" (cited in Kopp & Wegmann, 1988, p. 100). As Schleiermacher later put it in his lectures: "To dismember an act of speech into its individual parts is to make something indeterminate [*Unbestimmtes*]. Every individual sentence when ripped out of all context must be something indeterminate" (1977, p. 101).

Schleiermacher's work offers a useful framework for thinking about the problem of generalization when it comes to textual interpretation. It highlights, first and foremost, the concept of *understanding* as central to the practice of textual analysis. Schleiermacher's argument is that interpretation – which he explicitly calls an art because it cannot be "mechanized" – is nevertheless not a purely subjective or affective endeavor. Understanding something "correctly" implies that you can also *misunderstand* something. Even if there are no absolute right answers, truths for all time, there can be wrong answers. Accuracy, according to Schleiermacher, has an important place within the practice of textual analysis.

But Schleiermacher's work also codified for the first time that such understanding is conditional upon a simultaneous knowledge of part and whole. It does not say that textual critics can and should only focus on particulars. To the contrary, texts can *only* be understood (*kann nur verstanden werden*), according to Schleiermacher, through knowledge of the historical context in which an act of speech is produced. An exclusive focus on particulars does not lead to knowledge, but to indeterminacy and uncertainty (*etwas Unbestimmtes*).

What Schleiermacher's work does not do, however, is specify how knowledge of this whole is to be enacted or how it is then to be related to the particular act of speech that is being interpreted. Schleiermacher posits the necessity of this relationship – without the one we cannot understand the other – but he does not posit the method of its construction. How is one to construct a "totality" from specific examples? How is one to assess the exemplarity of an example?

In 1906, almost exactly one century after Schleiermacher's lectures on hermeneutics, Wilhelm Dilthey, just a few years prior to his death, published his short work, *Das Erlebnis und die Dichtung* [Poetry and Experience], in which he set out to tell a story in the tradition of the *grand récit* of the relationship between art and scientific knowledge. Dilthey was a direct inheritor of Schleiermacher's ideas, both a pastor's son and the author of a doctoral dissertation on Schleiermacher's ethics, written after being trained by two of Schleiermacher's students. As Chad Wellmon and Paul Reitter have shown, the terms that Dilthey established had a far-reaching impact on European and North American debates surrounding the self-justification of the humanities or *Geisteswissenschaften* (Wellmon & Reitter forthcoming 2021, chap. 4).

What interests me here is the way Dilthey's work both responds to and dramatically reverses Schleiermacher's model of the importance of generality for the purposes of textual understanding. For Dilthey, it was not a lifeworld that was essential for understanding any given act of speech. Rather, the selection of the *right* act of speech could be used – could only be used – as a vehicle for understanding one's lifeworld. The value of the arts and their study for Dilthey was that it was only *these* particulars that could lend insight into the largest of all possible generalities, which Dilthey called the "meaning of life." As Dilthey would write in highly evocative prose reminiscent of Lorenzo Valla:

> When memory, life experience and the thoughts that accompany them elevate the constellation of life, value, and meaning into something typical, when this experience becomes a vehicle and symbol of the universal and the goal and goods of the ideal, it is not knowledge of reality that appears in this universal vehicle of poetry, but the most vital experience of the relationship of our being to the meaning of life that finds expression. (1922, p. 179)

Here, a particular type of part – poetry, especially Romantic poetry, especially German Romantic poetry – is what allows access to knowledge not simply about the real world, but the meaning of our place within it (which Dilthey calls our *Daseinsbezüge*). In the face of Schleiermacher's lacuna – how was this whole to be conjured prior to knowledge of any given text – Dilthey turns things around so that all one needed was the right part to have access to the entire whole, "to discover the relationship of our being to the meaning of life." In place of a hermeneutics of the text, Dilthey substituted a hermeneutics of existence.

Dilthey's work was following in a long tradition of textual criticism that focused on a kind of "emulative" exemplarity – one reads classics because they represent in Mathew Arnold's words, the best of that which has been thought and said (Goldhill 2017). It was a fundamentally clerical model of criticism, one that relied on the moral authority of the critic to identify, preserve, and illuminate these canonical examples. But for Dilthey, exemplarity was no longer purely a matter of temporal and vertical striving, a vehicle used to emulate the greats of the past (the gods among us). It was a matter of detecting which works were the most successful (i.e., universal) in their ability to capture our existential enmeshment. Great works were the most general works.

Dilthey's work thus created a powerful paradigm through which hermeneutic attention to particulars could be seen as a vehicle to understanding the most general truths of our existence. In light of the growing empirical methods that Dilthey was observing all around him, Dilthey proposed an alternative avenue to generalization that, as we saw in Part II, is still operative today.

In the remainder of this section, I want to propose an alternative solution to the process of generalization, one that derives its inspiration from the work of the Open Science Collaboration and the values of transparency and openness that that work has inspired. Rather than argue for a state of exception for literary studies – that literary texts represent a special kind of object for which sample-based research is somehow inappropriate or that the knowledge of literary texts is somehow categorically different from other disciplines – I want to argue for a unified epistemological paradigm that applies across disciplines and across methodologies. In light of the prevalence and scale of generalization in our field, my argument is not that all research in literary studies ought to be sample-based and quantitative in nature. The reproducibility crisis has taught us that quantitative methods alone do not guarantee validity and reliability. Rather, my argument is that research in literary studies ought to adhere to the same principles of transparency, openness, and self-assessment with respect to the practice of generalization as other disciplines. Reproducibility remains in my view a core foundation of all knowledge production, though as I will show in Section 5, not the only one.

In a series of articles published in *Sociology*, first in 2000 and then in 2005 with Geoff Payne, Malcolm Williams proposed the idea of "moderate generalization" to address this problem within qualitative research in his field. As Williams claimed, "The interpretivist attitude to generalisation is rather like that of the Victorian middle classes towards sex. They do it, they know it goes on, but they rarely admit to either" (2000, p. 210).

Payne and Williams's goal was to make the practice of generalization in qualitative research more explicit. It was offered in response to quantitative critiques that one cannot reliably generalize from individual examples *at all*. Payne and Williams's argument was that qualitative research was an essential building block in the development and testing of theories at a more general level. Generalizations are poorer the less well they reflect the underlying world that they claim to represent. Knowledge of that world *in particular* is a key component of building better generalizations.

For Payne and Williams, the key to making qualitative research more credible was to follow the paradigm of "moderate" generalization, which they defined in the following way:

> They are moderate in two senses. First, the scope of what is claimed is moderate. Thus they are not attempts to produce sweeping sociological statements that hold good over long periods of time, or across ranges of cultures. Second, they are moderately held, in the sense of a political or aesthetic view that is open to change. This latter characteristic is important because it leads such generalizations to have a hypothetical character. They are testable propositions that might be confirmed or refuted through further evidence. (Payne & Williams 2005, p. 297)

For Payne and Williams, research based on small numbers of examples that aims to make generalizations should not encompass the sweeping spans of time that we saw in Part II (centuries, entire historical periods, modernity, the Anthropocene). But moderate generalizations should also be seen as moderately held in the sense of hypothetical. Moderate generalizations are in some sense nothing more than hypotheses generated from close contact with one's materials. These hypotheses can then be subject to further testing, not through more hand-selected and often biased examples, but through the collection of larger and more independent samples. Can we generalize from these samples and under what conditions? The work of the case study is to produce nuanced hypotheses about how texts work. The work of quantitative study is to test these hypotheses.

The second criterion of moderate generalization for Payne and Williams is that they ought to be explicit and projected throughout the research process:

> Although *moderatum* generalization is inherently modest, it cannot be taken to occur naturally and automatically in the process of doing research, or be left to the readers' discretion, or indeed, to the kinds of generalization that current qualitative researchers often seem to produce unconsciously. Research should be designed and undertaken in such a way that *moderatum* generalizations are consciously produced. (2005, p. 297)

It is not enough to simply assume the hypothetical nature of one's claims. The *telos* toward generality must be stated from the outset and the conditions of plausibility articulated. When researchers talk about "Victorian fiction" or "the *Bildungsroman*" or "scientific modernity," moderate generalization says that they also need to talk about the criteria under which those categories are being produced in their work. If I say explicitly, I am going to hypothesize that this single novel encapsulates an entire century's novelistic output and here are the reasons why, then I am engaging with the explicit project of generalization. It is also likely that I will begin to see the problematic leap of imagination that underlies this claim and thus will more naturally moderate the certainty with which I make it.

The work of Payne and Williams is valuable because it provides a series of criteria that we can apply across the board to both qualitative and quantitative research in the field of literary studies. It aims to undo the two-cultures nature of academic scholarship and provide a unified framework for assessing the relationship between evidentiary sufficiency and the scale, certainty, and extent of the claims being made in a given piece of research. While Payne and Williams use the term "moderate generalization" to refer to moderating the claims specifically of qualitative research, I would like to use the term "open generalization" instead to capture a larger process that one can apply to both forms of research. To engage in the practice of open generalization, then, means adhering to the following protocols:

1. Register the number of documents consulted.
When making a generalization, it is important to understand the relational nature of the observations from which the generalization has been derived.

Knowledge of how many, from where, in what format, and of what type needs to be made explicit when considering documents. In this Element, for example, I have accounted for exactly how many records have been consulted, where they came from, and why they were selected; how many individual examples have been martialed to illustrate my point within the text proper; whether those examples are indicative of generalization as well as its opposite (i.e., negative examples); and assessed the extent to which my insights about my topic may reasonably be extended to other documents given the variability and uncertainty within my observed data. Even when one is analyzing a single document, if the goal is to generalize about that work's exemplarity it must be made explicit in which context this exemplarity is valid. Such explicitness can help researchers assess how reasonable claims are, how much confidence we should endow the claims with and what plausible alternative scenarios may be. "After consulting two novels I conclude . . . " not only sounds different from "after consulting several hundred records . . . ." It helps draw attention to the implausibility of certain types of claims. It foregrounds the *relationship* between the scale of evidence and the scale of generalization as a key criteria of assessment.

2. Describe the criteria of selection.

Now that we know how big the sample was, we need to articulate the logic of its selection. In this Element, for example, I selected journal articles from two sets of journals, working from the assumption that they might behave differently with respect to my question. I also provided articles from outside of the field to provide contextual framing for whatever I might find within my field. Whenever we undertake a research project that aims to generalize, whether it is the "bibliographic imagination" or "modernist fiction," we need to ask ourselves why certain examples were chosen over others. Making this rationale explicit in advance helps guide the process of generalization as well as delimiting the boundaries of what can be claimed. "Given the documents I have chosen, I hypothesize that . . ." helps us see that this might also *not* be the case. No number of examples, however, will absolutely guarantee the validity of a generalization. We are always operating with uncertainty. While my sample is far larger than any used in the articles under study here, it does not encompass the entirety of the population about which claims are being made. The value of quantitative methods is the way they allow us to estimate and quantify that uncertainty, as well as allow others to reproduce and reassess those estimations. The openness of the process of selection allows other researchers to redo the process under the same or slightly altered conditions to assess just how much volatility there is in what is being estimated. It provides the ability to build social confidence in a belief about how the world works.

3. Examples should be illustrative not indexical.

To be clear, this Element is not a referendum on the value of examples (Felski 2017). Examples are the foundation of understanding. I have used examples liberally throughout. The point I want to make is *how* we use examples crucially matters to establish the credibility of the process of generalization. In other words, as I have tried to show throughout this Element, there are different kinds of examples. For my purposes here, I will discuss three. The first is what I call the "heuristic example": an example is used to *frame* a process of inquiry that will follow. An example of this type would be my use of Lorenza Valla. He is not used to prove anything about humanism but frames a way of inquiring into the nature of humanist discourse, for which future examples will be summoned that are meant to be representative of some larger social process. I could have chosen another example. Valla's value as an example is his ability to *clarify*, not prove. He is one among many.

The second type, what I call an "illustrative example," is one that is *supplementary* to some overall evidentiary practice. It helps illustrate some more general principle. It is avowedly partial, but also deictic – it points to the whole from which it is drawn and to which it belongs. There is nothing unique to the example other than it serves the purpose of making something "visible" or "graspable." It is intended to be "like" other examples. The numerous examples of generalization that I have used here are examples of this kind of exemplarity. Each illustrates another dimension or aspect of the same overall type, for which I could have chosen other examples. The illustrative example is one among many.

An "indexical example," on the other hand, does not illustrate something as a supplement but stands for it, *pars pro toto*. An indexical example is not part of the evidence but *is* the evidence. It represents the whole in the sense of standing for something that is not represented, or only represented *through it*. By way of example (!), consider the following two sentences:

36. Few texts [as Marinetti's manifesto] so effectively corroborate the view of fascism as a male fantasy, the martial mirage of an eroticism at last emancipated from affection and reproduction.

37. By understanding that relation, by conducting an atmospheric reading of *Jane Eyre*, we gain a more developed sense of how Victorian fiction understands and encodes climate.

Each of these sentences illustrates the use of indexical examples. Like illustrative examples, they stand for some larger whole (fascism or climate). But unlike the illustrative use of examples, they are not one example among many. They are the *only* piece of evidence, the whole for which they stand as part. Does Marinetti's work corroborate fascism as male fantasy more effectively than *almost all other* texts ever written? Can we be sure that *Jane Eyre* shows us how Victorian fiction understands climate or just how *Jane Eyre* understands climate? In the first case, Marinetti is exemplary, in the sense of distinctive, with respect to some imagined yet never invoked whole. In the second example, *Jane Eyre* is exemplary, in the sense of similar to, some imagined yet never invoked whole of Victorian fiction. In neither case is the exemplarity of the examples – their relationship to the whole to which they belong – put under scrutiny.

Exemplarity thus poses a basic representational problem. Examples stand in for something else. Evidentiary credibility is a function of the explicitness of this representational process, that is, when we explicate how an example is *like* something larger than itself rather than asserting that an example *is* something larger than itself. Exemplarity succeeds when we acknowledge and make explicit the chain of representations for which examples stand. In a quantitative framework, a single example (an observation) is used to represent a larger set of examples (a sample), which are in turn used to represent a larger whole for which they are claimed to stand (a population), whose relationship is mediated by another representation (a model). At every step, we are assessing the exemplarity of examples. Because we are always in a realm of representation, this chain can never be fully determined. There are always limitations and uncertainties to the exemplarity of examples. The *explicitness* of the relation is the crucial feature in determining values of confidence and credibility.

4. Incorporate limitations.

All of these gestures are meant to make the generalizing goals of an article more transparent and also more teleological – I have set out to argue something and have made the following choices to demonstrate it. But they will also have the residual effect of making the limits of our arguments more visible. Unlike other fields where "limitations" sections are mandatory, literary studies has no such codified practices. According to our sample of articles in this Element, articles almost uniformly do not invoke limitations. This is one more area where we need to break down the exceptionalism surrounding literary studies. We need to do a better job of explicitly gesturing toward the boundaries of how much we think we know: "I think this is true up to this point or under these conditions" also means saying I cannot be certain about these criteria or these conditions. This will inevitably help shrink the expanding world of claims we are making. Most of all, it will inject uncertainty into the research process, not as a rhetorical device – as when we use "perhaps," "it seems," "it appears that" – but as an explicit part of our methodology.

As I tried to demonstrate in Part II, one of the principal outcomes of following these guidelines is that literary scholarship will grow more uncertain. We will highlight as much what we do not know as what we do know. This will help undo the current ethos, where conviction rises in inverse relation to the copiousness of one's evidence. As the case study of Valla showed, the less evidence there is, the more rhetoric takes over. Rhetoric replaces evidence. The proposal for open generalization attempts to realign claim and evidence in a more positive way. The less there is, the less certain we are. Rhetoric reflects evidence.

Readers will likely sense a great deal of disenchantment in the face of these suggestions. As one reader of this Element suggested, this sounds awfully boring. It is! Generalizations should be boring, cautious, incremental, and slow. We have for too long substituted interestingness for evidence.

Readers will also likely be quick to point out that even if we do all of these things, spurious claims and unreliable generalizations will still be made. Look at other fields! This too is true. These steps are not guarantors of being "right," nor are they universal deterrents against being "wrong." Instead, they inject values of explication and openness into the process of adjudication. They move from a plane of individual right and wrong to one of collective confidence. Their value lies precisely in moving away from the certainty embodied by moral exemplarity to the uncertainty of collective belief. But of course we still might want to do away with all this truth-talk entirely.

5 Don't Generalize (at All): The Case for the Open Mind

In his defense of aesthetic judgment, Kant bases the deduction of this uniquely human faculty on a useful fiction: "The judgment of taste determines its object through its consideration of a sense of delight (as beauty) with a claim to everyone's agreement, *as though* it were objective [*Das Geschmacksurteil bestimmt seinen Gegenstand in Ansehung des Wohlgefallens (als Schönheit) mit einem Anspruche auf jedermanns Beistimmung, als ob es objektiv wäre*]" (1996, p. 210, my emphasis). For Kant, judgments of taste are not just fundamentally subjective. They desire objectivity. They are in their nature designed to seek out agreement or *Beistimmung* with another person. When we experience something beautiful, we imagine this experience not just to be shareable, but universal, something that everyone surely must also be feeling. In the moment of beauty, there lies a desire for communion.

However subtle, Kant's "as if" has had massive repercussions for the history of literary studies. Even more radical than Valla's position that rhetoric and proof are necessarily intertwined, Kant's suggestion is that there can be no empirical agreement when it comes to matters of taste. All judgments of this kind are particular, but particular in a way that we want them to be general: "Thus all judgments of taste are also particular judgments because they combine their predicate of delight not with a concept, but with a single given empirical projection [*Daher sind auch alle Geschmacksurteile einzelne Urteile, weil sie ihr Prädikat des Wohlgefallens nicht mit einem Begriffe, sondern mit einer gegebenen einzelnen empirischen Vorstellung verbinden*]" (1996, p. 220).

As is well known, Kant's aim was to open up a space of human experience that was outside the dictates of "understanding." For Kant, aesthetic experience marked a distinctly different form of mental activity. Aesthetic experience was for Kant about allowing for, legitimizing, the place of desire within human thought. It was about rejecting that ideas or *Begriffe* were associated with aesthetic experience. Instead, it foregrounded the value of what he saw as a synthetic form of thought, one that brought together feeling and object into a higher union. Aesthetic experience cultivated what Kant called "empirical imaginations [*empirische Vorstellungen*]," singular, object-bound cognitions that were not generalizable. Where Schleiermacher saw the goal of textual criticism as one of understanding, for Kant the goal of a particular type of textual engagement, that is, texts that appealed to our senses and imagination, was the cultivation of a particular synthetic faculty, the combination of affect and object.

However impactful Kant's work has been, we have arguably never taken it quite literally enough. In the incessant drum of generalizations uttered in textual research about creative works that we saw in Part II, we have clearly overlooked Kant's argument about the inherent fictionality of our insights. We have taken "concrete singular empirical imaginations" and turned them into generalizable concepts about works of art. This is exactly what, according to Kant, we were *not* supposed to do. What was universal for Kant was our capacity to judge, not the individual contents of the judgment. We have treated these useful fictions as though they were true.

Kant's work is not alone in making this assertion. In Kant's wake would emerge a long tradition of thought that was deeply critical of the generalizing dimension of textual interpretation, from Friedrich Nietzsche's belief in textual truth as an "army of metaphors," to Schleiermacher's successor Hans-Georg

Gadamer's (1990) emphasis on the time-bound and thus experiential nature of interpretive truth, to Stanley Fish's (1976) argument that textual truths are a function of interpretive communities and not the texts themselves, to the more recent work of Rita Felski (2008, 2015) and the affective turn that aims to move beyond what Felski calls a "hermeneutics of suspicion" and toward readers' emotional connections with texts as a core aspect of understanding textual meaning. According to this tradition, the notion that there is some kind of textual truth that could be "independent" of the observer, or in the words of the OSC, independent of "the authority and motivations of the source," is a logical fallacy.

In this section, I want to take this Kantian-inspired position seriously and entertain the idea that we should *never* generalize when it comes to making statements about texts, or at least a particular subset of them, those that make a claim to some kind of aesthetic experience. Rather than translate our subjectivities into generalizations *as if* they were objective (much as Fish did about "the reader" even as he made claims for the impossibility of generalization with respect to texts), we should instead acknowledge and foreground that every observation we make is explicitly only valid "for me."

The first problem that emerges with such a thought-experiment is that it would require a massive rewording of our writing on a scale potentially even greater than the transformations I outlined in Section 4. If moderating our generalizations within explicit limitations will require vast new kinds of rhetorical and methodological effort, so too will the suppression of generalization itself. If one out of every two or three statements in the framing of a research article is a generalization, we are looking at a good deal of behavioral change to bring this program to fruition.

The second problem is more nuanced. Let's assume for a moment that generalization as a practice disappeared. What or whom would all of these subjective responses be for? What is the *good* of undoing the fictional objectivity of our insights? Why would we maintain a system that consists solely of the expression of singular imaginations on the part of publicly and privately subsidized individuals?

Kant's answer to this question is somewhat complicated in detail (not surprisingly) but more straightforward if we take a somewhat general view (there it is again). Kant strings together aesthetic judgment with aesthetic production through the figure of the "genius," the creator who creates according to his own natural rules. Were the genius to create according to inherited rules, these would impose "concepts" onto the creative process and thus lack connection with one's aesthetic sense and its fundamental independence from understanding. Genius according to Kant is "the exemplary originality of the natural gift of a subject in the free use of his capacity for understanding [*die musterhafte Originalität der Naturgabe eines Subjekts im freien Gebrauche seiner Erkenntnisvermögen*]." Kant continues, "In this way the product of a genius is not an example of imitation, but the cause for another genius who will be awoken to the feeling of his own originality [*Auf solche Weise ist das Produkt eines Genies ... ein Beispiel nicht der Nachahmung ... sondern der Nachfolge für ein anderes Genie, welches dadurch zum Gefühl seiner eigenen Originalität aufgeweckt wird*]" (1996, p. 55).

And there you have it. "Genius" is something that is not imitated but *produced* in a chain reaction of artistic creation. Genius causes more genius. It magnifies freedom and originality. The source of genius is aesthetic judgment. We teach works of art and write about our own individual judgments, because in doing so we amplify the amount of freedom and originality in the world. What better justification do we need than that?

It is important to emphasize that this is a huge and as yet untested hypothesis. But it is also important to emphasize just how much this view departs from the current refrain of disciplinary justification that one often hears in the field and that revolves around the concept of "critical thinking." Kant's answer, by contrast, is far different and I would argue far more profound: experience of the arts creates more freedom in the world.

Here, I want to offer a slight variation (and moderation) of Kant's argument. In keeping with the ethos of this Element, I am also going to try to validate it using a larger sample of data. The argument I want to make is that the insights generated from engagements with works of art – in this case literature, but potentially expandable to all the arts – do not produce greater amounts of "freedom" (*pace* Kant), but what I will call "conceptual openness" or the "open mind." The value of such conceptual openness – and this is my untested hypothesis – is that it can inform richer and more nuanced generalizations and theories about how the world *might* work in two different senses: first, in the sense of tentativeness, as we hypothesize about the world, and second, in the sense of alternativeness, as we imagine different worlds altogether. Where Kant's answer was an end in itself – individual judgments are expressions of freedom, thus more of them equals more freedom – my answer is more circular. Conceptual openness is not an end in itself but can be a valuable foundation of the process of generalization and understanding the world. This too is a large and as yet untested hypothesis. In what follows, I want to at least begin the process of justifying the belief in the conceptual openness produced by the field of literary studies as something distinctive to it. Generalizing is not the only thing that research in literary studies does.

"le suggérer ... voila le rêve" - Mallarmé

After writing two books on medieval literature and philosophy, Umberto Eco changed course and in 1962 published a book about contemporary art and the idea of "the open work" (Eco 1989). For Eco, recent musical experiments by composers like Karlheinz Stockhausen or Henri Pousseur offered a new framework for thinking about the aesthetics of openness and the receptive mentalities that such openness made possible. In Stockhausen's *Klavierstück XI*, for example, the performer was presented with a single large sheet of paper with groupings of notes. The performer would then choose where to begin and how to concatenate the groups to compose their own musical narrative.

Such musical experiments were by the 1960s the most explicit attempts to empower a viewer, listener, or reader to engage the work with as much freedom as possible. But they were part of a long line of aesthetic activity that for Eco largely began in the modernist period, with notable examples by Joyce or Mallarmé. (In 1962, this observation still felt fresh.) As Eco quotes Pousseur on the value of this kind of work:

> Since the phenomena are no longer tied to one another by a term-to-term determination, it is up to the listener to place himself deliberately in the midst of an inexhaustible network of relationships and to choose for himself, so to speak, his own modes of approach, his reference points and his scale, and to endeavor to use as many dimensions as he possibly can at the same time and thus dynamize, multiply, and extend to the utmost degree his perceptual faculties. (1989, p. 10)

Eco would call this type of work "the work in movement," and since his book appeared, we have seen numerous celebrations of the kind of open-ended creative work that he was initially celebrating. Indeed, electronic or algorithmic literature was in many ways thought to be this tradition's direct inheritor.

In this section, I want to claim Eco's concept of the "open work" as an object of value not only in the aesthetic realm but also the critical realm as well. As Eco would argue, "indeterminacy is a valid stepping stone in the cognitive process" (1989, p. 15). The open work for Eco led to the open mind. It allowed one, in the words of Pousseur, to "extend to the utmost degree one's perceptual faculties." More recent research has begun to show the value of ambiguity, uncertainty, and openness when it comes to human thought and experience. Uncertainty not only leads to more cognitive arousal; it can also lead to more social engagement and collaborative problem solving (Schultz et al. 2008, Uchiyama et al. 2012). As Peter McMahan and James Evans (2018) have argued, we have for too long undervalued the work of ambiguity in scholarly and critical thinking:

Generations of natural and social scientists claimed that precise language would enable critical evaluation of truth claims, accelerate scientific discovery, and facilitate the accumulation of knowledge through reproducible description. Precision would coordinate the rationality of scientific investigation. Ambiguity, by contrast, was accused of impeding high-fidelity communication by failing to maintain a sharp boundary between truth and fiction, information and emotion, substance and style, and so increased the flow of false information. (2018, p. 862)

The work of McMahan and Evans shows instead that ambiguity can be a useful "boundary object" that "leads to individual and collective uncertainty about communicated meanings in academic discourse. Uncertainty drives social interaction and friction, which yields coordination ... . Ambiguous words and phrases allow ideas to travel further" (p. 894). When it comes to scholarly expression, the emphasis on ambiguity and uncertainty, rather than precision and proof, allows for a different kind of generality to take place. Instead of a controlled model of increasingly universal statements that encloses more particular ones – a kind of enclosure model of generalization – the open work initiates a more uncontrolled or stochastic expansionism. It allows for the emergence of new and unexpected contexts for ideas, surprising combinations, but also adaptations. As McMahan and Evans write, as ambiguous ideas travel, "they are transformed by new, receiving audiences, and word meanings are adapted to fit local, representational needs and circumstances" (p. 870). Ambiguous expression makes new things happen.

One of the ways openness has been championed within academic circles is through the notion of "access." Openness makes academic writing more accessible. While this can refer to the removal of material prohibitions surrounding the accessibility of documents – pay walls, subscriptions, and copyright – it can also refer to discourse. There is a longstanding critique of textual studies' inaccessibility as a function of it being too technical or "jargony." As defenders often point out, the same critiques are not leveled at the sciences. There is an implicit expectation that writing about writing, as opposed to writing about natural or social phenomena, should be more open in terms of its rhetorical accessibility to general audiences.

I mention this because it is precisely not the kind of openness I mean here. My understanding of openness derives from Eco and the tradition he gestures toward, where openness is a quality that challenges expectations and norms. Being open in this sense does not mean being more *easily* accessible. Rather, being open for Eco means undoing familiarity and certainty.

In the space remaining, I am going to make the case that literary studies embodies three kinds of expressive openness and that this openness ought to be more centrally foregrounded and celebrated within the discipline. In other words, there is a particular set of values of openness that, like generalization, are intrinsic to the discipline and that, like generalization, we ought to be more explicit about our enactment of them.

To understand the prevalence of these behaviors within literary studies, I am going to compare the sample of articles from the field of literary studies discussed in Part II with two other samples that I have created for my purposes here. The first is a collection of 832 book reviews published in the popular Canadian publication *Quill and Quire*, between 2015 and 2017. The aim in choosing this corpus is to observe a set of documents that is similarly concerned with literature but is written for a public-facing forum. The second set is a collection of 150 articles published in 2016 drawn from three journals in the field of cell biology (*Journal of Cell Biology, Molecular and Cellular Biology,* and *BMC Biology*). The aim of this collection is to provide a representation of science writing that is sampled in similar ways to our literary studies articles. While different scientific disciplines will exhibit different kinds of linguistic behavior – worth further study – here I want to provide a single comparison point for language drawn from the natural sciences with respect to literary studies.

The three values of openness that I am going to argue and test for here are what I will call the questioning mind, the expanding mind, and the loosening mind. By the *questioning mind*, I mean a rhetorical stance that is at once both critical and open. It doubts but also wonders. This is what Susan Wolfson calls the "interrogative mode," which she derives from the poet John Keats's emphasis on our "negative capability" (1986). Interrogation or negation is not meant in a forensic sense of insisting on finding out the truth or denying its existence. Instead, this mode prizes uncertainty and the duration of incompletion.

There are many ways in which this mode may be embodied in scholarly writing. The simplest and most straightforward way to measure it is through the presence of questions themselves. The more questions we ask, the less space we have to answer them, and the more we embrace Wolfson's ideal of "the questioning presence." As it turns out, articles in literary studies do tend to ask significantly more questions than scientific writing, which seldom asks questions within the scope of an article (Figure 6a). In other words, *the performance of questioning* is a value that the study of literature brings into public view. It is part of the rhetoric of explanation and description when it comes to the study of texts.

The second value of openness I refer to is the *expanding mind*. One way to think of this is as the valuation of the "novel" or "unforeseen," things that have not been thought before. The aspects of surprise, that is, the unforeseenness of words, and semantic richness, that is, the diminishment of repetition within our vocabulary, could be used as two correlates for this idea. Using the measures of "surprisal" and "type-token ratio" respectively, we can see how literary studies produces language that is less surprising than scientific writing and yet lexically richer (Figure 6b-c).[4] At the same time, we might also think about the idea of "expansion" as a function of "length," where the placement of pressure on expectations about quantitative limits serves as the ground of opening up. As we can also see from Figure 6(d-e), literary studies exhibits significantly longer words as well as sentences. Indeed, sentences in literary studies are on average about 25% longer than sentences one might find in science journals.

As Stefania Degaetano-Ortlieb et al. (2018) have demonstrated, what makes scientific writing so hard to understand from a lay reader's perspective is its divergence from customary uses of language. It represents a highly specialized form of language, one that looks more repetitive but also more surprising when compared to other fields. What makes literary studies challenging, by contrast, is its divergence from *stylistic* norms. Literary studies is expansive in that it seeks out concepts that take up more literal space, that alphabetically occupy our minds, but also in the way these articles expand the duration of an idea in the grammatical space of the sentence, much as this sentence has done. Writing about creative texts is intended not to be novel in the sense of coining new terms, but expansive and challenging in the sense of opening-up space for thinking while reading. Rather than codify or taxonimize the world in more definitive terms, it *goes on.*

The final form of openness that I want to advocate for is what I will call the *loosening mind.* For me, this refers to a capacity to undo associations and make room for novel connections. As I mentioned earlier, this depends less on the inventiveness of novel terms than it does on the undoing of fixed associations with existing terms. The loosening mind recontextualizes and remixes. The loosening mind is also the folding mind, turning things over and making new forms.

One way we can think to capture the degree to which literary studies is marked by this practice is to observe the level of semantic concentration within articles. By semantic concentration, I mean the extent to which key terms are framed in more concentrated and unchanging ways – there is more predictability to the language associated with key terms or concepts in the field. In literary studies, these key terms might be "novel," "human," or "language"; in book reviews, "book," "story," or "readers"; and in biology, it might be "cells," "expression," and "genes." Semantic concentration does not focus on the frequency of these

---

[4] Type-token ratio calculates the average number of word instances (types) over the total number of words (tokens). My implementation takes 100 samples of 100-word passages to avoid problems with the differential lengths of texts. For surprisal, I implement the model described by Stefania Degaetano-Ortlieb and Elke Teich (2017).

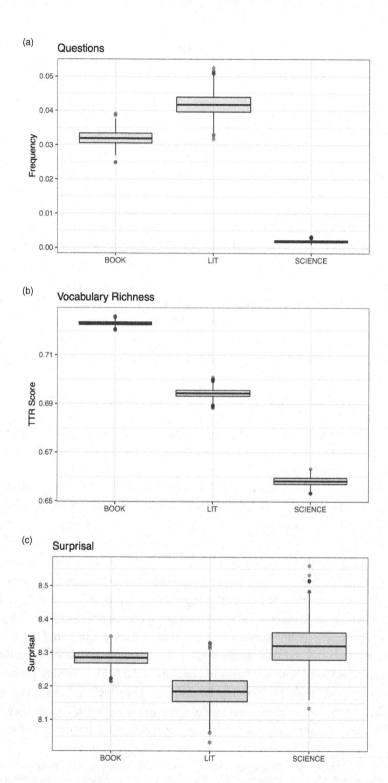

Figure 6 Average percentage of questions, vocabulary richness, surprisal, sentence, and word length based on 1,000 bootstrap samples per field.

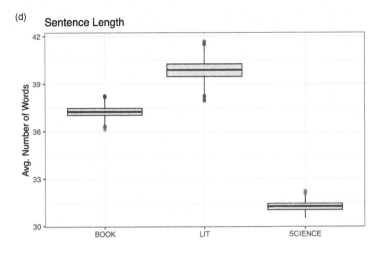

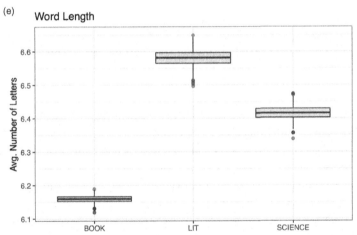

Figure 6 (cont.)

terms but instead the frequency of co-occurring terms that appear alongside them. How much diversity is there when we talk about novels or language in our field compared to when biologists speak of genes or expressions?

To calculate this, I use a measure called a "concentration ratio." Economists often use concentration ratios to assess the degree of monopolization within an industry. A CR10, for example, would calculate the percentage of market share that the top ten companies in a given industry account for. The higher the number, the more concentration there is and the less diversity. In my case, a CR10 calculates the percentage of total words that the top ten most frequently co-occurring words account for around a particular keyword. The more often a

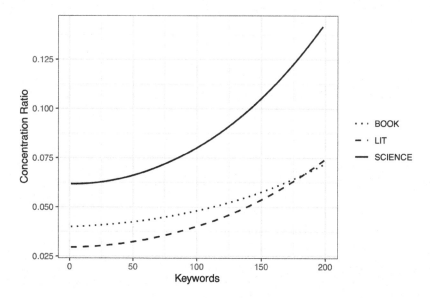

Figure 7 Semantic concentration using CR10 for the top 200 most frequent
words per field (N=1,110).

few words account for most of the words surrounding a key term, the more
semantic concentration there is. Thus a score of 0.20 means that the 10 most
frequently co-occurring words around a keyword account for 20% of all occur-
rences of co-occurring words. ("Co-occurring" is defined in this case as words
that appear within +/− 9 words of the keyword.) The more concentrated the
distribution for each keyword, the more semantic concentration there is around
core concepts in the field and, it is assumed, the lower levels of openness and
ambiguity.

As we can see in Figure 7, there is a dramatic difference with respect to the
degree of semantic concentration between science writing and literary studies.
Two-cultures seems like a reasonable way to describe this linguistic behavior.
Contrary to the surprisal and vocabulary richness scores noted earlier, here we
see how scientific writing invests far more heavily in a controlled vocabulary
around key terms. The repetition of terms around keywords is drastically higher
in scientific articles than either book reviews or literary scholarship. The median
value of concentratedness in scientific articles is just under twice the level of
literary studies. Interestingly, the concentration is lowest in literary studies
overall. The median value of semantic concentration in book reviews is higher
than almost three-quarters of the key terms in literary studies, suggesting that
one of the core values of literary studies is a more open use of language in
general when talking about literature.

These are just some of the ways that the value of openness – here understood not as material or discursive accessibility, but as a form of rhetorical questioning, loosening, and expanding – are distinctly exhibited within the field of literary studies. These are characteristics that make literary studies unique relative to other kinds of writing. If the practice of generalization is what makes research in literary studies similar to other fields, the rhetorical practices of questioning, expanding, and loosening are at least some of the qualities that make literary studies distinctive from other fields. It is important that we not only see both of these dimensions but that we imagine some way forward where the two work in concert rather than in opposition, or as in Valla, simply as substitutions for each other.

Conclusion

On the Mutuality of Method

In this Element, I have tried to show both the prevalence and semantic nature of generalization in the field of literary studies. According to the evidence provided here, I estimate that between one out of every two to three sentences in the opening and closing frames of research articles in the field contains a generalization. These levels appear to be roughly commensurate with quantitative research methods as exhibited by the sample of sociology articles. While we do see some important differences between different kinds of journals – field-specific articles tend to have lower rates of generalization than generalist journals – overall their rates are similar enough to suggest that there is field-wide consistency when it comes to the practice of generalization irrespective of researcher type.

Going further into the data, I also tried to highlight the scales at which literary studies operates, that is, to explicate the nature and scope of generalization when it is happening. Even though generalizations appear to be highly prevalent in the field, one might believe that these are likely to be more modest or at smaller scales than quantitative fields working with much greater amounts of evidence. On the contrary, according to our sample of data, the language most indicative of generalizing statements in literary studies disproportionately contains references to large-scale "literary," "cultural," "modern," or "human" behavior. Literary studies does not shy away from working with the most general categories possible. Indeed, we saw a descending order of generality when it came to the framework of time in our articles. Where literary studies focuses the most on the "modern," history works with the "century," and sociology attends to the "year." There appears to be an inverse relationship between the scale of claims and scope of evidence provided.

In addition to this analysis, I also tried to highlight the evidentiary lacunae that such generalizations can entail with respect to the manual sorting of evidence. Generalizations serve as unproven and untested evidentiary short-hands to justify interpretive conclusions that have not been rigorously subject to scrutiny. In Section 4, "The Case for Open Generalization," I tried to list a variety of practices that we can engage in to subject our generalizations to greater transparency and, one hopes, to help moderate the scale, scope, and frequency of their occurrence.

At the same time, I have also tried to draw attention to a very different research practice, one that goes back to the work of one of the founding figures of humanism, Lorenzo Valla, and what I call the work of "the open mind." This too draws on values of openness inspired by the open science movement. Rather than celebrate transparency as the sole ideal of research, however, it emphasizes conceptual and intellectual openness as important complements as well. My aim here has been to use the empirical methods afforded by the advances in machine learning and natural language processing to valorize the rhetorical and theoretical creativity of literary scholarship. We do not only generalize. Creative theoretical constructs are every bit as important in *expanding* our modeling of the world as principles of transparency are for improving the *credibility* of our modeling.

In identifying these two strands within our research, my aim has been to reframe their relationship not as one of opposition or substitution, but of mutuality. Without empirical methods, we will never be able to validate the social value of our investment in conceptual openness other than through recourse to our own authority. On the other hand, all of the transparency in the world will never by itself allow us to discover anything novel and meaning-ful about the world. Without the creativity and flexibility incubated by the methods of the open mind, we will go on seeing the same thing over and over again, much like what Plato said about writing's invention in the first place.

At the same time, we cannot continue to substitute interestingness for evidence and maintain our credibility as a discipline. We need to do a better job of foregrounding theorizing as theoretical and generalizing as an empirical prac-tice, one that requires more reflection on the sufficiency of evidence informing the claims being made, as well as the theoretical richness of the framework being applied. What is required is a greater clarity of purpose, as well as mutuality of method. Rather than focus on being right or wrong in the absolute sense, or disavowing these categories altogether, we can strive to build confi-dence in our collective forms of knowledge about the world all the while continuing to imagine alternative versions. Maybe *versioning* might be the best way to capture this idea: the practice of turning scholarly vision around on itself in a continual practice of imaginative self-awareness.

References

Ash, M., Herndon, T., & Pollin, R. (2013). Does high profile debt consistently stifle economic growth? A critique of Reinhart and Rogo. *Political Economy Research Institute Working Paper Series*, no. 322.

Baggerly, K. A. & Coombes, K. R. (2009). Deriving chemosensitivity from cell lines: Forensic bioinformatics and reproducible research in high-throughput biology. *Annals of Applied Statistics*, 3, 1309–1344. https://doi.org/10.1214/09-AOAS291

Berkeley, G. (1710). *A Treatise Concerning the Principles of Human Knowledge*, London: Printed for Jacob Tonson.

Bode, K. (2018). *A World of Fiction: Digital Collections and the Future of Literary History*, Ann Arbor: University of Michigan Press.

(2020). Why you can't model away bias. *Modern Language Quarterly*, 81(1), 95–124. https://doi.org/10.1215/00267929-7933102

Bossaerts, P., Camerer, C., Fiorillo, C. D. et al. (2008). Explicit neural signals reflecting reward uncertainty. *Phil. Trans. R. Soc. B.*, 363, 3801–3811. https://doi.org/10.1098/rstb.2008.0152

Bourrier, K. & Thelwall, M. (2020). The social lives of books: Reading Victorian literature on Goodreads. *Journal of Cultural Analytics*. https://doi.org/10.22148/001c.12049

Bowersock, G. W. (2008). Introduction. In L. Valla, *On the Donation of Constantine*, trans. G. W. Bowersock, Cambridge, MA: Harvard University Press.

Buurma, R. S. & Heffernan, L. (2012). The common reader and the archival classroom: Disciplinary history for the twenty-first century. *New Literary History*, 43(1), 113–135. https://doi.org/10.1353/nlh.2012.0005

Camporeale, S. I. (1996). Lorenzo Valla's oratio on the pseudo-donation of Constantine: Dissent and innovation in early Renaissance humanism. *Journal of the History of Ideas*, 57(1), 9–26. https://doi.org/10.2307/3653880

Contessa, G. (2007). Scientific representation, interpretation, and surrogative reasoning. *Philosophy of Science*, 74(1), 48–68. https://doi.org/10.1086/519478

Degaetano-Ortlieb, S., Hannah, K., Khamis, A., & Teich, E. (2018). An information-theoretic approach to modeling diachronic change in scientific English. *From Data to Evidence in English Language Research*. Suhr, C., Nevalainen, T., & Taavitsainen, I. (Eds.), Leiden: Brill. 258–281.

Degaetano-Ortlieb, S. & Piper, A. (2019). The scientization of literary study. *Proceedings of the 3rd Joint SIGHUM Workshop on Computational Linguistics for Cultural Heritage, Social Sciences, Humanities and Literature*, 18–28. https://doi.org/10.18653/v1/W19-2503

Degaetano-Ortlieb, S. & Teich, E. (2017). Modeling intra-textual variation with entropy and surprisal: Topical vs. stylistic patterns. *Proceedings of the Joint SIGHUM Workshop on Computational Linguistics for Cultural Heritage, Social Sciences, Humanities and Literature*, 68–77. https://doi.org/10.18653/v1/W17-2209

Devlin, J., Chang, M-W., Lee, K., Toutanova, K. (2019). BERT: Pre-training of Deep Bidirectional Transformers for Language Understanding. *Proceedings of NAACL-HLT*, 4171–4186.

Dilthey, W. (1922). *Das Erlebnis und die Dichtung. Lessing, Goethe, Novalis, Hölderlin*, 8th ed., Wiesbaden: Springer.

Earp, B. D. & Trafimow, D. (2015). Replication, falsification, and the crisis of confidence in social psychology. *Frontiers in Psychology.* https://doi.org/10.3389/fpsyg.2015.00621

Eco, U. (1989). *The Open Work*, Cambridge, MA: Harvard University Press.

Emre, M. (2018). *Paraliterary: The Making of Bad Readers in Postwar America*, Chicago: University of Chicago Press.

Erickson, L. & Thiessen, E. D. (2015). Statistical learning of language: Theory, validity, and predictions of a statistical learning account of language acquisition. *Developmental Review*, 37, 66–108. https://doi.org/10.1016/j.dr.2015.05.002

Evans, J. A. & Foster, J. G. (2011). Metaknowledge. *Science*, 331(6018), 721–725. https://doi.org/10.1126/science.1201765

Evans, J. A. & McMahan, P. (2018). Ambiguity and engagement. *American Journal of Sociology*, 124(3), 860–912. https://doi.org/10.1086/701298

Felski, R. (2008). *Uses of Literature*, Malden, MA: Blackwell Publishing.
  (2015). *The Limits of Critique*, Chicago: University of Chicago Press.
  ed. (2017). Special issue: For example. *New Literary History*, 48(3), 415–608.

Fish, S. E. (1976). Interpreting the "Variorum." *Critical Inquiry*, 2(3), 465–485. https://doi.org/10.1086/447852

Fohrmann, J. & Voßkamp, W. eds. (1994). *Wissenschaftsgeschichte der Germanistik im 19. Jahrhundert*, Stuttgart: Metzler.

Foster, E. D. & Deardorff, A. (2017). Open Science Framework (OSF). *Journal of the Medical Library Association: JMLA*, 105(2), 203–206. https://doi.org/10.5195/jmla.2017.88

Gadamer, H.-G. (1990). *Wahrheit und Methode: Grundzüge einer philosophischen Hermeneutik*, Tübingen: Mohr.

Gius, E., Reiter, N., & Willand, M. (2019). Foreword to the Special Issue: "A shared task for the digital humanities: Annotating narrative levels," *Journal of Cultural Analytics*. https://doi.org/10.22148/16.047

Gladen, B. & Rogan, W .J. (1978). Estimating prevalence from the results of a screening test. *American Journal of Epidemiology*, 107(1), 71–76. https://doi.org/10.1093/Oxfordjournals.Aje.A112510

Goldhill, S. (2017). The limits of the case study: Exemplarity and the reception of classical literature. *New Literary History*, 48(3), 415–435. https://doi.org/10.1353/nlh.2017.0023

Goldstone, A. & Underwood, T. (2014). The quiet transformations of literary studies: What thirteen thousand scholars could tell us. *New Literary History*, 45(3), 359–384. https://doi.org/10.7282/T3222RZT

Grafton, A. (1994). *Defenders of the Text: The Traditions of Scholarship in an Age of Science, 1450–1800*, Cambridge, MA: Harvard University Press.

Grafton, A. & Jardine, L. (1986). *From Humanism to the Humanities: Education and the Liberal Arts in Fifteenth- and Sixteenth-Century Europe*, Cambridge, MA: Harvard University Press.

Guillory, J. (1993). *Cultural Capital: The Problem of Literary Canon Formation*, Chicago: University of Chicago Press.

Guo, P., Ma, Z., & Stodden, V. (2013). Toward reproducible computational research: An empirical analysis of data and code policy adoption by journals. *PLOS ONE*, 8(6), e67111. https://doi.org/10.1371/journal.pone.0067111

Hacking, I. (1999). *The Social Construction of What?* Cambridge, MA: Harvard University Press.

Harada, T., Koeda, T., Ohno, K. et al. (2012). Distinction between the literal and intended meanings of sentences: A functional magnetic resonance imaging study of metaphor and sarcasm. *Cortex*, 48(5), 563–583. https://doi.org/10.1016/j.cortex.2011.01.004

Hayot, E. (2016). Against historicist fundamentalism. *PMLA*, 131(5), 1414–1422. https://doi.org/10.1632/pmla.2016.131.5.1414

Horvat, M., Mlinarić, A., & Smolčić, V. S. (2017). Dealing with the positive publication bias: Why you should really publish your negative results. *Biochemia medica*, 27(3), 030201. https://doi.org/10.11613/BM.2017.030201

Hunter, M. C. (2010). Experiment, theory, representation: Robert Hooke's material models. In Frigg, R. & Springer, H., *Beyond Mimesis and*

Convention: Representation in Art and Science, Dordrecht: Springer Science+Business Media, 193–219.

Iqbal, F., Binsalleeh, H., Fung, B. C. M., & Debbabi, M. (2013). A unified data mining solution for authorship analysis in anonymous textual communications. *Information Sciences*, 231, 98–112. https://doi.org/10.1016/j.ins.2011.03.006

Jameson, F. (1986). Third world literature in the era of multi-national capitalism. *Social Text*, 15, 65–88. https://doi.org/10.2307/466493

Kant, I. (1996) *Kritik der Urteilskraft*, Frankfurt/Main: Suhrkamp.

Kelley, D. R. (1970). *Foundations of Modern Historical Scholarship: Language, Law, and History in the French Renaissance*, New York: Columbia University Press, 19–46.

Kopp, D. & Wegmann, N. (1988). Wenige wissen noch, wie Leser lieset.' Anmerkungen zum Thema: Lesen und Geschwindigkeit. In Oellers, N., ed. *Germanistik und Deutschunterricht im Zeitalter der Technologie: Selbstbestimmung und Anpassung*, Tübingen: Niemeyer, 92–104.

Laplace, P. S. (1841). Mémoire sur la probabilité des causes par les évènements. *Oeuvres complètes*, 8, 27–65.

Lerer, S. (2002). *Error and the Academic Self: The Scholarly Imagination, Medieval to Modern*, New York: Columbia University Press.

Levine, C. (2017). Model thinking: Generalization, political form, and the common good. *New Literary History*, 48(4), 633–653. https://doi.org/10.1353/nlh.2017.0033

Locke, J. (1824). *Essay Concerning Human Understanding*, 12th ed., London: Rivington.

Martinez-Fuentes, C. & Vicente-Saez, R. (2018). Open Science now: A systematic literature review for an integrated definition. *Journal of Business Research*, 88, 428–436. https://doi.org/10.1016/j.jbusres.2017.12.043

Nauta, L. (2009). *In Defense of Common Sense: Lorenzo Valla's Humanist Critique of Scholastic Philosophy*, Cambridge, MA: Harvard University Press.

Nelson L. D., Simmons, J. P. & Simonsohn, U. (2011). False-positive psychology: Undisclosed flexibility in data collection and analysis allows presenting anything as significant. *Psychological Science*, 22(11), 1359–1366. https://doi.org/10.1177/0956797611417632

Open Science Collaboration. (2012). An open, large-scale, collaborative effort to estimate the reproducibility of psychological science. *Perspectives on Psychological Science*, 7(6), 657–660. https://doi.org/10.1177/1745691612462588

(2015). Estimating the reproducibility of psychological science. *Science*, 349, 6251. https://doi.org/10.1126/science.aac4716

Payne, G. & Williams, M. (2005). Generalization in qualitative research. *Sociology*, 39(2), 295–314. https://doi.org/10.1177/0038038505050540

Peters, M.E., Neumann M., Iyyer, M., Gardner, M., Clark, C., Lee, K., Zettlemoyer, L. (2018). Deep contextualized word representations. *Proceedings of NAACL-HLT*, 2227–2237. https://doi.org/10.18653/v1/N18-1202

Piper, A. (2017). Think small: On literary modeling. *PMLA*, 132(3), 651–658. https://doi.org/10.1632/pmla.2017.132.3.651

Piper, A. & Sachs, J. (2018). Technique and the time of reading. *PMLA*, 133(5), 1259–1267. http://doi.org/10.1632/pmla.2018.133.5.1259

Piper, A. & Wellmon, C. (2017). Publication, power and patronage: On inequality and academic publishing. *Critical Inquiry*. http://criticalinquiry.uchicago.edu/publication_power_and_patronage_on_inequality_and_academic_publishing/

Polanyi, M. (2009). *The Tacit Dimension*, Chicago: University of Chicago Press.

Popper, K. (1935). *Logik der Forschung. Zur Erkenntnistheorie der modernen Naturwissenschaft*, Wien: Springer.

Porter, T. M. (1986). *The Rise of Statistical Thinking, 1820–1900*, Princeton: Princeton University Press.

Reichenbach, H. (1930). Kausalität und Wahrscheinlichkeit. *Erkenntnis*, 1, 158–188. https://doi.org/10.1007/BF00208615

Reynolds, L. D. & Wilson, N. G. (1991). *Scribes and Scholars: A Guide to the Transmission of Greek and Latin Literature*, 3rd ed., Oxford: Clarendon Press.

Rogan, W. J. & Gladen, B. (1978). Estimating prevalence from the results of a screening test. *American Journal of Epidemiology*, 107(1), 71–76.

Rogers, D. (1650). *Naaman the Syrian, His Disease and Cure*, London: Printed by Th. Harper for Philip Nevil.

Rudin, C. (2019). Stop explaining black box machine learning models for high stakes decisions and use interpretable models instead. *Nature Machine Intelligence*, 1, 206–215. https://doi.org/10.1038/s42256-019-0048-x

Schleiermacher, F. (1977). *Hermeneutik und Kritik*, Frankfurt/Main: Suhrkamp.

Schultz W., Preuschoff K., Camerer C., Hsu M., Fiorillo C.D., Tobler P.N. and Bossaerts P. (2008). Explicit neural signals reflecting reward uncertainty. *Phil. Trans. R. Soc. B*, 363: 3801–3811. https://doi.org/10.1098/rstb.2008.0152

Shapin, S. (1994). *A Social History of Truth: Civility and Science in Seventeenth-Century England*. Chicago: University of Chicago Press.

So, R. J. (2017). All models are wrong. *PMLA*, 132(3), 668–673. https://doi.org/10.1632/pmla.2017.132.3.668

Spellman, B. (2015). A short (personal) future history of revolution 2.0. *Perspectives on Psychological Science*, 10(6), 886–899. https://doi.org/10.1177/1745691615609918

Stigler, S. (1986). *The History of Statistics Before 1900*, Cambridge, MA: Belknap Press.

Thiessen, E. D. (2017). What's statistical about learning? Insights from modelling statistical learning as a set of memory processes. *Phil. Trans. R. Soc. B.*, 372, 20160056.

Uchiyama, H. T., Saito, D. N., Tanabe, H. C., Harada, T., Seki, A., Ohno, K., Koeda, T., & Sadato, N. (2012). Distinction between the literal and intended meanings of sentences: a functional magnetic resonance imaging study of metaphor and sarcasm. *Cortex*, 48(5), 563–583. https://doi.org/10.1016/j.cortex.2011.01.004

Underwood, T. (2016). *Why Literary Periods Mattered*, Stanford: Stanford University Press.

Valla, L. (2008). *On the Donation of Constantine*, trans. G. W. Bowersock. Cambridge,MA: Harvard University Press.

Viswanathan, G. (1989). *Masks of Conquest: Literary Study and British Rule in India*, New York: Columbia University Press.

Wellmon, C. & Reitter, P. (forthcoming 2021). *Permanent Crisis: The Humanities in a Disenchanted Age*, Chicago: University of Chicago Press.

Williams, M. (2000). Interpretivism and generalisation. *Sociology*, 34(2), 209–224. https://doi.org/10.1177/S0038038500000146

Willinsky, J. (2006). *The Access Principle: The Case for Open Access to Research and Scholarship*, Cambridge, MA: MIT Press.

Wolfson, S. J. (1986). *The Questioning Presence: Wordsworth, Keats, and the Interrogative Mode in Romantic Poetry*, Ithaca: Cornell University Press.

Cambridge Elements ☰

Digital Literary Studies

Katherine Bode
Australian National University

Katherine Bode is Professor of Literary and Textual Studies at the Australian National University. Her research explores the critical potential and limitations of computational approaches to literature, in publications including *A World of Fiction: Digital Collections and the Future of Literary History* (2018), *Advancing Digital Humanities: Research, Methods, Theories* (2014), *Reading by Numbers: Recalibrating the Literary Field* (2012) and *Resourceful Reading: The New Empiricism, eResearch and Australian Literary Culture* (2009).

Adam Hammond
University of Toronto

Adam Hammond is Assistant Professor of English at the University of Toronto. He is author of *Literature in the Digital Age* (Cambridge 2016) and co-author of *Modernism: Keywords* (2014). He works on modernism, digital narrative, and computational approaches to literary style. He is editor of the forthcoming *Cambridge Companion to Literature in the Digital Age* and *Cambridge Critical Concepts: Literature and Technology*.

Gabriel Hankins
Clemson University

Gabriel Hankins is Associate Professor of English at Clemson University. His first book is *Interwar Modernism and the Liberal World Order* (Cambridge 2019). He writes on modernism, digital humanities, and color. He is technical manager for the Twentieth Century Literary Letters Project and co-editor on *The Digital Futures of Graduate Study in the Humanities* (in progress).

About the Series

Our series provides short exemplary texts that address a pressing research question of clear scholarly interest within a defined area of literary studies, clearly articulate the method used to address the question, and demonstrate the literary insights achieved.

Cambridge Elements ≡

Digital Literary Studies

Elements in the Series

Can We Be Wrong? The Problem of Textual Evidence in a Time of Data
Andrew Piper

A full series listing is available at: www.cambridge.org/EDLS

Printed in the United States
By Bookmasters